Getting to Know the United States

OUR CONSTITUTION, OUR GOVERNMENT

Robert James Field

BOOK LAB

PO Box 230206, New York, NY 10023-0206

Table of Contents

1

A Snapshot
of Our Country

KEY WORDS

election — A system in which voters select a person to represent them.
The voters select the mayor of the city in the *election*.

veteran — A person who was in the army, navy, marines, or air force.
The *veteran* fought in the Civil War.

minimum wage — The lowest wage that is legal.
Most businesses must pay *minimum wages*.

rights — Those things that are due to you as a citizen of a country.
We have the *rights* of life, liberty, and the pursuit of happiness.

insure — To promise to pay people back if they lose money or property.
The government *insures* people's money in most banks.

federal government — Our Country's government.
The United States government.
The main offices of the *federal government* are in Washington, D.C.

WHO ARE THE AMERICAN PEOPLE?

Who are the American people?

Americans are people whose families came from hundreds of places to get to the United States. Millions of people came here from all over the world.

Our families arrived here from all parts of Europe and Asia. They came from Africa and South America. Many traveled thousands of miles in crowded and dirty ships to get here.

Americans are people of all religions. Our country allows people to choose their own religion. Christians, Jews, and Moslems live side by side in our land.

Why did so many people want to come to our country? What magic does the name "American" have? Our study of the Constitution will help us answer these questions.

Freedom

Freedom is an idea. You cannot touch freedom. You cannot see it, smell it, or hear it. But you *can* feel it!

2

You feel it when you see a picture of the Statue of Liberty. You feel pride when you see the White House or the Capitol Building in Washington, D.C. You share these feelings with all Americans.

We enjoy many rights by living in the United States. Sometimes we take these rights for granted. We forget that most people in the world do not have our freedom.

Our government sees that we all have civil rights. This means that we are all equal under the law. We are free to go about our business as long as we do not bother others.

These civil rights give Americans great freedom to be what they want. No wonder so many people wanted to make the long and hard trip to the United States!

We choose our leaders

American people choose their own leaders. They do this by peaceful elections. The people who are elected to be our leaders choose others to help them run the government. These are called *appointments*.

American people are the real bosses. Our leaders must please the voters. Otherwise they will not keep their jobs.

Other benefits

We cannot even list *all* of the benefits that we get from our country. Here are just a few of them:

Education

Our country has always believed in public education. We have a long history of helping our people get an education.

All Americans have the right to go to a public school. A public school is a school that is paid for by taxes. It is open to all people. Our nation's government works with the states and the cities. The government makes sure that all of our citizens have good schools.

For many years, our government helped people who were in the armed services go to college. Otherwise, many of them could not afford to go to college.

Our Court System

Our court system protects our rights. If we are blamed for a crime and we did not do it, we are protected. We are innocent until we are proved guilty.

The courts are separate from the other branches of government. This makes sure that the other branches do not get too strong.

Welfare of Less Fortunate People

The government gives poor people a helping hand. The government also helps children and adults of all ages.

3

Our government takes money from our paychecks for SOCIAL SECURITY. Our employer also pays for our Social Security. This money goes to the government. We get it back when we retire.

If we lose our job, we get money from the government to help us live. This is called UNEMPLOYMENT COMPENSATION. It is paid from a tax on employers.

The government gives food stamps to poor families to help them. Poor mothers with small children get special aid to help the children.

Help With Our Jobs

The federal government helps us when we work. Laws protect small children from hard work. Other laws set up a MINIMUM WAGE.

The federal government makes sure that we do not have to work too many hours or work in a place that is too dangerous.

Mail Service

Our mail service is the United States Postal Service. It serves everybody. No town is too small to have its own post office. The RURAL FREE DELIVERY service delivers farmers' mail to their homes.

Defense

Our government helps us keep our freedoms with a strong defense team. The army, navy, marines, and air force are there to help us. They are like a fire department. We hope that we will not have to use them. But it is nice to know that they are there. They will help if we need them.

Public Health

In the United States each person may choose a doctor. But the federal government helps our doctors and hospitals.

The PUBLIC HEALTH SERVICE works with research groups to protect us from disease.

The FOOD AND DRUG ADMINISTRATION (FDA) must test all new drugs. This is to stop harmful drugs from being sold. The FDA also sees that the drugs really work.

Money

Most people know that the federal government prints paper money and makes our coins. But the government also protects our money in many ways.

The FEDERAL RESERVE SYSTEM watches the thousands of banks in our country. It makes sure that the banks take good care of our money.

The government has an agency that *insures* the money that we put into our bank accounts. A special sign (seal) on the door tells us that the bank is *insured*. If anything happens to our money in the bank, the government will give us our money back.

Space Research

We can be proud of our record in space travel.

Space travel is so new that we still do not know all the good it can do. Scientists developed better watches, calculators, and more powerful computers from their space research. Many scientists believe that better medicines will be developed in space laboratories.

Some Other Services

The government helps us with weather reports. It makes sure that we can enjoy good radio and TV programs. The FBI protects us from kidnappers and criminals. Inventors and authors are protected by patents and copyrights. The COAST GUARD saves many lives each year by watching our lakes and seas.

These are just some of the many ways that the government touches our lives. It would take a big book to list all of them. You will learn more about them as you study the Constitution.

THE LIBERTY BELL

CHAPTER 1

What Did You Learn?

ONE: VOCABULARY

1. Use the key words to complete the paragraph.

election   veteran

minimum wage   rights

insure   federal government

We have a _____ _____ in the United States.

The government gives us many _____ because we live in a

free country. The government helps us in many ways. If we have money in a

bank, the government _____s our bank account. Our government

sees that we earn enough money by making a _____ _____. The

country helps people who were in the armed forces. These _____s

get many benefits.

2. Read each sentence. Write the word which best completes the meaning of the sentence.

1. A _____ is someone who was in the army.   [veteran, vitamin]

2. The federal government prints and coins _____.   [matches, money]

3. The _____ keeps us safe from kidnappers and criminals.   [FBI, FDA]

4. We have a _____ government.   [foreign, federal]

5. _____ protect inventors.   [Pencils, Patents]

6

TWO: UNDERSTANDING THE FACTS

1. Fill in the right words.

1. _____ protects our bank accounts if the bank loses our money.

       A. A school   C. Insurance
       B. A mayor   D. The Army

2. The _____ _____ saves many lives each year on our lakes and seas.

       A. Coast Guard   C. President
       B. Post Office   D. Law Service

3. The F.D.A. sees that our _____ are safe.

       A. children   C. pets
       B. bank accounts   D. drugs

4. We are _____ until we are proved to be guilty.

       A. jailed   C. angry
       B. innocent   D. taxed

5. _____ _____ helps us to pay our bills when we get too old to work.

       A. The FBI   C. The Defense Department
       B. Social Security   D. The Post Office

2. True or False?

Circle T or F:

1. The government helped veterans go to college.   T   F
2. Space research only helps our space program.   T   F
3. Our leaders have to please us.   T   F
4. The court system helps us to keep our rights.   T   F

3. Write a paragraph:

How does the United States government help you?

_____

_____

_____

_____

_____

_____

THREE: LEARNING THE LANGUAGE

When did it happen?

Present tense = today or every day.   Past tense = yesterday.

Example:

PRESENT TENSE	PAST TENSE
This year we choose our leaders in the election.	We chose our leaders in the election four years ago

1. I _____ _____ at   I _____ _____ at
   7:00 every day.   7:00 yesterday.

   (wake up, woke up)

2. I _____ to school.   I _____ to school.

   (went, go)

3. I _____ my teacher.   I _____ my teacher.

   (see, saw)

4. I _____ my hair.   I _____ my hair.

   (brushed, brush)

5. I _____ my   I _____ my
   homework.   homework.

   (do, did)

8

PLEDGING ALLEGIANCE

2

How to Be a Citizen

KEY WORDS

alien — A person who lives in a country but is not a citizen.
Juanita was born in Mexico. Now she lives in the United States.
She is an *alien* until she becomes a citizen.

full partner — Somebody who shares all of the rights in a group.
A citizen is a *full partner* of our country.

citizen — Someone who is a member of a country. A full partner in our country.
A person is a *citizen* if he or she is born in our country.
People who are not born in the United States can also become *citizens*.

naturalized citizen — A foreign born person who becomes a citizen.
Marie was born in France. When she first came to the United States she was an alien.
She became a *naturalized citizen* by studying and following the laws.

Everybody who lives in the United States is either a *citizen* or an *alien*. Most people who live in the United States want to be a *full partner* in our country. They want to share all of the benefits of their country. A person must be a *citizen* to share *all* of these benefits.

Who is a citizen?

All people born in the United States are citizens. People who are born in Puerto Rico are citizens. This is because Puerto Rico is a part of the United States.

A child who is born in another country is a citizen if his or her parents are American citizens.

Children under 18 who live in the United States are citizens if their parents *become* citizens.

An alien may become a citizen by following certain rules. This is called *naturalization*.

How an alien becomes a citizen

A person who is an alien may become a citizen. He or she becomes a *naturalized citizen*. People who want to become *naturalized citizens* must follow these rules.

They must be 18 years old or older.

They must show that they speak and understand common English words.

They must live in the United States for 5 years. (But a husband or wife of an American citizen only has to live here 3 years.)

They must show that they are honest and that they obey the law.

They must know about American history.

They must show that they understand the United States Constitution. It is very important to understand the Constitution if you want to become a citizen.

People who become *naturalized citizens* have all of the rights of those who are born here. *EXCEPT* — They may not become President or Vice President of the United States.

Naturalized citizens are proud when they become citizens. They had to study. They did not become citizens just because they were born here.

Naturalized citizens give our country much of its flavor. They come from all over the world. Many of them do great things for the United States.

CHAPTER 2

What Did You Learn?

ONE: VOCABULARY

1. Write a sentence using each key word. Study the key words on page 10 if you need help.

aliens	full partner
citizen	naturalized citizen

1. _____

2. _____

3. _____

4. _____

2. Read each sentence. Write the beginning letter that gives the underlined word meaning.

1. All people born in the United States are _____ itizens. [c, t]

2. _____ aturalized citizens are aliens who become citizens. [P, N]

3. Naturalized citizens have almost all of the _____ ights
   of those who were born here. [r, p]

4. Naturalized citizens cannot be _____ resident. [S, P]

TWO: UNDERSTANDING THE FACTS

1. Fill in the right words.

1. A person must be _____ years old to become a naturalized
   American citizen.

   A. 10   C. 18
   B. 21   D. 5

2. Everybody who lives in this country is either a

citizen or an _____ .

      A. eagle   C. apple
      B. alien   D. animal

3. Children under 18 years old who live in the United States are

_____ if their parents become citizens.

      A. aliens   C. poor
      B. adults   D. citizens

4. An alien must know about American history and the

_____ to become a citizen.

      A. Constitution   C. rules for driving a car
      B. newspaper   D. name of a lawyer

2. True or False?

Circle T or F:

1. An alien is always a creature from outer space.   T F
2. Puerto Ricans are citizens of our country.   T F
3. A person who wants to be a naturalized citizen of our country must speak perfect English.   T F
4. All persons born in the United States are citizens.   T F

THREE: LEARNING THE LANGUAGE

Change each question into a statement.

Example: QUESTION — Are all people born in the United States citizens?

      STATEMENT — All people born in the United States are citizens.

1. QUESTION — Was Andrea born in Canada?

    STATEMENT — _Andrea w born in Canada_

13

2. QUESTION — Is a citizen a member of a country?

   STATEMENT — _____

3. QUESTION — Is Puerto Rico part of the United States?

   STATEMENT — _____

4. QUESTION — Is it very important to understand the Constitution?

   STATEMENT — _____

3

An Introduction to the
U.S. Constitution:

KEY WORDS

Congress — The group of people who make our country's laws.
Congress passed a law that helps the workers.

preamble — A statement that tells us the purpose of the Constitution.
The *preamble* tells us why we need the Constitution.

privilege — A special right given to some people.
Voting is a *privilege* that citizens have.

dictator — A head of a country who has all of the power.
Dictators can do whatever they want. People have few rights and no freedom in
countries ruled by *dictators*.

What is a Constitution?

We must know what a *constitution* is before we can study the United States
Constitution.

The United States Constitution is a PLAN for our government. It tells us
what kinds of laws our government can make.

When we study the United States Constitution, we do *not* study *all* of the laws of the country. That would take many thousands of books.

We study the *types* of laws that the United States government can pass.

The Constitution also tells us how the government is set up. We will see that the power of the government is cut into three parts — the President — the Congress — the courts. This makes sure that no one group has all the power.

Why our country needs a Constitution

Here is a good way to understand why the country needs a constitution. Think of a club that you might want to start. Compare the club to a country. The club needs rules just as a country needs laws.

When you decide what kind of rules you need for your club, you can write a type of constitution.

For example, what if only two club members hold a meeting? Do you think that it is fair if they pass laws that the whole club would have to obey?

The United States constitution has a rule for this. It stops just a few congressmen from passing laws for the whole Congress.

How would the Constitution help you run your club?

A club needs a leader. The president of the club is the leader.

Do you want the club president to do whatever he or she wants? Do you think that there must be some control over what the president does? If the leader has complete control, this is like a dictator.

Presidents of the United States cannot do whatever they want. The Constitution tells what powers the President has. The President must obey the Constitution.

What is the purpose of the club?

The purpose of the club can be told in a short message that comes before the club constitution. There *is* a message like this before our country's Constitution. It is called the *preamble*.

Think of a small club as we study the United States Constitution.

This helps you to understand it better. The ideas are the same even though the country has over two hundred million people and your club might have only ten members.

How can a 200-year-old Constitution still work today?

If we look at the important countries in the world, our country is one of the newest. But it has one of the oldest governments.

Our country's power comes from the people. Most of the people long ago agreed to obey the Constitution's ideas. Since then most people think that it is working fine. So we still agree to obey its rules.

Our Constitution is almost two hundred years old. But it has only 26 official changes.

When the Constitution was written, the fastest way to travel was by horse. This was also the fastest way of sending news to another person.

Now we have things that the writers of the Constitution never knew. We have space travel and computers. We have radio, television, and telephones.

If someone long ago said that you could look at a box to see and hear things from many miles away, people would think that the person was crazy!

What would people in those days think of going to the moon or talking into a machine to someone hundreds of miles away? They could never dream of traveling in a carriage without a horse. They did not think of many other things that we are used to.

The people who wrote the Constitution did not dream of these things! But the Constitution that they wrote is still strong and good for our modern problems. We shall see how and why this is so.

Why do we study the Constitution?

Most of us can vote when we are eighteen years old or become a citizen. That is one of the great privileges which we have in a free country.

In order to be a smart voter, you must know how your government works. You should also learn about your rights and the responsibilities that go with those rights.

THE PEOPLE WHO WROTE THE CONSTITUTION DID NOT DREAM OF THESE THINGS

CHAPTER 3

What Did You Learn?

ONE: VOCABULARY

1. Use the key words to complete each sentence.

       privilege   preamble

       Congress   dictator

   1. The _____ is the statement that tells us the purpose of the Constitution.   [product, preamble]

   2. _____ is the group of people who make our country's laws.   [Congress, College]

   3. A _____ has all of the power in a country.   [doctor, dictator]

   4. Voting is a _____ that citizens have.   [privilege, poem]

2. Crossword. Fill in the blanks from the following words. Use the definitions to help you.

congress   rights
dictator   privilege
Constitution

DEFINITIONS

Across

1. A plan for our government.

2. We have these because we live in a free country.

Down

3. The group of people who make our laws.

4. A special right given to some people.

5. The head of a country who has all of the power.

TWO: UNDERSTANDING THE FACTS

1. Fill in the right word.

    1. The Constitution is a _____ for our government.

          A. state   C. play
          B. movie   D. plan

    2. _____ is a privilege that citizens over 18 have.

          A. Watching television   C. Sleeping
          B. Voting   D. Reading

    3. The _____ is a statement that tells us why we need the Constitution.

          A. preamble   C. income tax
          B. newspaper   D. article

    4. _____ are rulers of a country who have all of the power and can do whatever they want.

          A. Mayors   C. Governors
          B. Dictators   D. Vice Presidents

    5. The President must _____ the United States Constitution.

          A. obey   C. erase
          B. write   D. forget

2. True or False?

Circle T or F:

1. The Constitution is a list of all of the country's laws.	T	F
2. The country's power comes from the people.	T	F
3. The national government has three main parts.	T	F
4. The preamble is at the end of the Constitution.	T	F
5. There are 26 official changes to the Constitution.	T	F

3. Write a paragraph:

Write a short paragraph telling why our country needs a Constitution.

_____

_____

_____

_____

_____

_____

THREE: LEARNING THE LANGUAGE

Making new words. Compound words. Compound words are two words put together to make a new word.

1. Circle each word in these compound words:

Example: (good) (night)

1.	whatever	6.	baseball
2.	Congressman	7.	bookcase
3.	cannot	8.	afternoon
4.	someone	9.	cowboy
5.	without	10.	pancake

2. Add another word to each word to make a compound word:

Example: sun + shine = sunshine.

1. some _____
2. no _____
3. book _____
4. house _____
5. fire _____

21

4

How Our Country Began

KEY WORDS

colony — A country or land that is owned and run by another country.
Mexico was a Spanish *colony*.

colonist — A person who lives in a country that is run by another country.
George Washington was a *colonist* of England before the United States became a country.

trade — Business or commerce.
The United States and Japan *trade* with each other.

representation — Having someone in government who looks out for your interests.
The colonists had no *representation* in the English government.

independence — Freedom.
We celebrate our country's *independence* on July 4.

rebel — A person who fights against one's own government.
The *rebel* fought to overthrow the government.

revolution — A rapid and sudden change.
   Everything changes with the *revolution*.

Revolutionary War — The war that we fought for independence from England.
   George Washington was the main general in the *Revolutionary War*.

A time machine

A time machine is a machine in science fiction. It takes a person ahead or back in time.

Pretend that we have a time machine. Our first stop is in 1492. Here is what we see.

New land for countries in Europe

Christopher Columbus wants to find a shorter way to go to India. People want to go to India because of its spices and riches. India is east of Europe. It is a long and hard trip to go from Europe to India.

Columbus thinks that the world is round. He thinks that it would be easier to go west to India.

At first he cannot get money for this trip because most people think that he is foolish. They think that the world is as flat as a pancake. They fear that anybody who sails too far falls off the edge of the world.

At last Queen Isabella of Spain gives Columbus the money for his trip. After many weeks of rough sailing, the crew finds land. Everybody is happy because they think the land they see is the East Indies.

But Columbus' discovery is even greater! He finds a whole new "world."

After Columbus discovers the new world, the important European countries try to get as much of this land as they can. This new land is in North, Central, and South America. New land means new riches for the European countries.

Colonies

The countries that take over land call their new land a colony. Spain, France, and England start many colonies in the new world.

England owns all thirteen colonies after the French and Indian War in 1759. More and more English people come to the colonies to get a new start in life.

How England treats its Colonists

At first England treats its colonists fairly. But England's battle with the French and Indians costs her a lot of money. The English king tries to get back as much money as he can from the colonists.

The colonists pay more and more for their goods. England buys most of the raw materials from the colonies at low prices. They sell the colonists finished goods at high prices.

What made the Colonists angry?

The colonists' taxes get higher and higher. They also do not have any "say" in their government. Nobody looks after their rights in England. These two things make the colonists very upset and angry.

The Boston Tea Party

Tea is the most important drink for the colonists. Most of the colonists were born in England. That is why they have English habits. Tea is as popular for adults as coffee is now.

When England puts a huge tax on tea, the colonists start the famous Boston Tea Party. Colonists dress as Indians and creep upon a ship in the Boston Harbor. They throw tons of tea overboard.

This makes the King angry. He gets even tougher with the colonists. But very few colonists want to rebel and split away from England. All they want is to get a fair deal from England.

When things get worse, more colonists start to complain about how they are treated. Now more of them openly talk about rebellion. The King's actions make the same colonists stick together in their anger.

The Revolutionary War

The Revolutionary War soon becomes a sure thing. It is a long and bloody war.

England is one of the strongest countries in the world. The English think that they can win the war quickly. But the colonists' strong beliefs and anger help them defeat the British. Then they declare their independence.

CASE 1

England Is Unfair

PROBLEM:

England has to pay for the huge costs of the French and Indian War.

BACKGROUND:

At first England is fair to the colonists, but then England tries to make the colonists pay for the costs of the wars and the upkeep of the colonies.

Choose the right word or words for each blank.

      sell   England   high   taxes

SOLUTIONS:

England: 1. Raises the colonists' _____.

            2. Charges the colonists _____ prices for goods that they buy.

            3. Pays the colonists lower prices for raw materials that the

               colonists _____ to_____.

25

High Taxes Anger the Colonists

PROBLEM:
The colonists start to feel that they are cheated because of the high taxes.

BACKGROUND:
The colonists have no representation (voice) in the English government. But they have to pay very high taxes to England.

Choose the right word or words for each blank.

    Boston Tea Party   England   better

SOLUTIONS:

1. The colonists start to plan ways to make England treat

   them _____.

2. The _____ _____ _____
   is staged as a protest.

3. The colonists and _____ go to war.
                  (Revolutionary War)

CHAPTER 4

What Did You Learn?

ONE: VOCABULARY

1. Use the key words to complete the sentences.

> HINT —To find a meaning of a word you do not know, look at the words around the unknown word. Other words may help you find the meaning.

1. Mexico was owned by Spain. Mexico was a _____.
   - A. continent
   - B. colony
   - C. language
   - D. dictator

2. The United States and Japan sell things to each other. They

   _____ with each other.
   - A. play
   - B. eat
   - C. argue
   - D. trade

3. George Washington fought against England when England was his

   country. He was a _____.
   - A. rebel
   - B. sailor
   - C. writer
   - D. poet

4. The colonists fought the English to gain their freedom. They fought the

   _____ War.
   - A. Revolutionary
   - B. Civil
   - C. Trade
   - D. Legal

5. The United States won its freedom from England. Now the United States

   was _____.

       A. weak   C. lost

       B. independent   D. flat

2. Can you unscramble these words?

   1. BLERE _____   Someone who fights against his or her own government.

   2. YLONOC _____   A country that is run by another country.

   3. EDART _____   Business or commerce.

   4. NDPEDECINENE _____   Freedom of action or thought.

HINTS

independence   rebel

trade   colony

TWO: UNDERSTANDING THE FACTS

1. Put these events in the right order:

_____ A. The Revolutionary War begins.

_____ B. Columbus discovers the "new world."

_____ C. The Boston Tea Party is held.

_____ D. England charges the colonists higher taxes.

2. Fill in the right words.

1. _____ did not have colonies in the new world.

    A. Liberia   C. England
    B. France   D. Spain

2. _____ made many colonists angry with England.

    A. The English language   C. Cold weather
    B. Too much freedom   D. High taxes

3. Many colonists thought that England was _____.

    A. unfair   C. too kind
    B. in Asia   D. afraid

4. The _____ was held to protest high taxes on tea.

    A. Boston Tea Party   C. train
    B. Commonwealth   D. celebration

5. The troubles the colonists had with England caused the _____.

    A. War of 1812   C. Good feelings
    B. Revolutionary War   D. Representation

3. True or False?

Circle T or F:

1. At first England treated the colonists fairly.   T   F
2. The colonists had many people to represent them in England.   T   F
3. Tea was very important for the colonists at the time of the Boston Tea Party.   T   F
4. The Boston Tea Party made King George happy.   T   F

THREE: LEARNING THE LANGUAGE

Base words. We use base words with different endings to make new words.

Base Word	New Words	
1. revolt	revolution	revolutionary
2. colony	colonist	colonial
3. represent	representation	representative
4. Independent	independence	independently

Use one of the word forms in each sentence.

1. We fought the R _____ War.

2. The colonies won their i_____ from England.

3. George Washington was a c_____ of England before the Revolutionary War.

4. The colonists had no r _____ in the English government.

A DECLARATION

BY THE REPRESENTATIVES OF THE

UNITED STATES OF AMERICA,

IN GENERAL CONGRESS ASSEMBLED.

WHEN in the Course of human Events, it becomes necessary for one People to dissolve the Political Bands which have connected them with another, and to assume among the Powers of the Earth, the separate and equal Station to which the Laws of Nature and of Nature's God entitle them, a decent Respect to the Opinions of Mankind requires that they should declare the causes which impel them to the Separation.

We hold these Truths to be self-evident, that all Men are created equal, that they are endowed by their Creator with certain unalienable Rights, that among these are Life, Liberty, and the Pursuit of Happiness—That to secure these Rights, Governments are instituted among Men, deriving their just Powers from the Consent of the Governed, that whenever any Form of Government becomes destructive of these Ends, it is the Right of the People to alter or to abolish it, and to institute new Government, laying its Foundation on such Principles, and organizing its Powers in such Form, as to them shall seem most likely to effect their Safety and Happiness. Prudence, indeed, will dictate that Governments long established should not be changed for light and transient Causes; and accordingly all Experience hath shewn, that Mankind are more disposed to suffer, while Evils are sufferable, than to right themselves by abolishing the Forms to which they are accustomed. But when a long Train of Abuses and Usurpations, pursuing invariably the same Object, evinces a Design to reduce them under absolute Despotism, it is their Right, it is their Duty, to throw off such Government, and to provide new Guards for their future Security. Such has been the patient Sufferance of these Colonies; and such is now the Necessity which constrains them to alter their former Systems of Government. The History of the present King of Great-Britain is a History of repeated Injuries and Usurpations, all having in direct Object the Establishment of an absolute Tyranny over these States. To prove this, let Facts be submitted to a candid World.

He has refused his Assent to Laws, the most wholesome and necessary for the public Good.

He has forbidden his Governors to pass Laws of immediate and pressing Importance, unless suspended in their Operation till his Assent should be obtained; and when so suspended, he has utterly neglected to attend to them.

He has refused to pass other Laws for the Accommodation of large Districts of People, unless those People would relinquish the Right of Representation in the Legislature, a Right inestimable to them, and formidable to Tyrants only.

He has called together Legislative Bodies at Places unusual, uncomfortable, and distant from the Depository of their public Records, for the sole Purpose of fatiguing them into Compliance with his Measures.

He has dissolved Representative Houses repeatedly, for opposing with manly Firmness his Invasions on the Rights of the People.

He has refused for a long Time, after such Dissolutions, to cause others to be elected; whereby the Legislative Powers, incapable of Annihilation, have returned to the People at large for their exercise; the State remaining in the mean time exposed to all the Dangers of Invasion from without, and Convulsions within.

He has endeavoured to prevent the Population of these States; for that Purpose obstructing the Laws for Naturalization of Foreigners; refusing to pass others to encourage their Migrations hither, and raising the Conditions of new Appropriations of Lands.

He has obstructed the Administration of Justice, by refusing his Assent to Laws for establishing Judiciary Powers.

He has made Judges dependent on his Will alone, for the Tenure of their Offices, and the Amount and Payment of their Salaries.

He has erected a Multitude of new Offices, and sent hither Swarms of Officers to harrass our People, and eat out their Substance.

He has kept among us, in Times of Peace, Standing Armies, without the consent of our Legislatures.

He has affected to render the Military independent of and superior to the Civil Power.

He has combined with others to subject us to a Jurisdiction foreign to our Constitution, and unacknowledged by our Laws; giving his Assent to their Acts of pretended Legislation:

For quartering large Bodies of Armed Troops among us:

For protecting them, by a mock Trial, from Punishment for any Murders which they should commit on the Inhabitants of these States:

For cutting off our Trade with all Parts of the World:

For imposing Taxes on us without our Consent:

For depriving us, in many Cases, of the Benefits of Trial by Jury:

For transporting us beyond Seas to be tried for pretended Offences:

For abolishing the free System of English Laws in a neighbouring Province, establishing therein an arbitrary Government, and enlarging its Boundaries, so as to render it at once an Example and fit Instrument for introducing the same absolute Rule into these Colonies:

For taking away our Charters, abolishing our most valuable Laws, and altering fundamentally the Forms of our Governments:

For suspending our own Legislatures, and declaring themselves invested with Power to legislate for us in all Cases whatsoever.

He has abdicated Government here, by declaring us out of his Protection and waging War against us.

He has plundered our Seas, ravaged our Coasts, burnt our Towns, and destroyed the Lives of our People.

He is, at this Time, transporting large Armies of foreign Mercenaries to compleat the Works of Death, Desolation, and Tyranny, already begun with circumstances of Cruelty and Perfidy, scarcely paralleled in the most barbarous Ages, and totally unworthy the Head of a civilized Nation.

He has constrained our fellow Citizens taken Captive on the high Seas to bear Arms against their Country, to become the Executioners of their Friends and Brethren, or to fall themselves by their Hands.

He has excited domestic Insurrections amongst us, and has endeavoured to bring on the Inhabitants of our Frontiers, the merciless Indian Savages, whose known Rule of Warfare, is an undistinguished Destruction, of all Ages, Sexes and Conditions.

In every stage of these Oppressions we have Petitioned for Redress in the most humble Terms: Our repeated Petitions have been answered only by repeated Injury. A Prince, whose Character is thus marked by every act which may define a Tyrant, is unfit to be the Ruler of a free People.

Nor have we been wanting in Attentions to our British Brethren. We have warned them from Time to Time of Attempts by their Legislature to extend an unwarrantable Jurisdiction over us. We have reminded them of the Circumstances of our Emigration and Settlement here. We have appealed to their native Justice and Magnanimity, and we have conjured them by the Ties of our common Kindred to disavow these Usurpations, which, would inevitably interrupt our Connections and Correspondence. They too have been deaf to the Voice of Justice and of Consanguinity. We must, therefore, acquiesce in the Necessity, which denounces our Separation, and hold them, as we hold the rest of Mankind, Enemies in War, in Peace, Friends.

We, therefore, the Representatives of the UNITED STATES OF AMERICA, in GENERAL CONGRESS, Assembled, appealing to the Supreme Judge of the World for the Rectitude of our Intentions, do, in the Name, and by Authority of the good People of these Colonies, solemnly Publish and Declare, That these United Colonies are, and of Right ought to be, FREE AND INDEPENDENT STATES; that they are absolved from all Allegiance to the British Crown, and that all political Connection between them and the State of Great-Britain, is and ought to be totally dissolved; and that as FREE AND INDEPENDENT STATES, they have full Power to levy War, conclude Peace, contract Alliances, establish Commerce, and to do all other Acts and Things which INDEPENDENT STATES may of right do. And for the support of this Declaration, with a firm Reliance on the Protection of divine Providence, we mutually pledge to each other our Lives, our Fortunes, and our sacred Honor.

Signed by ORDER and in BEHALF of the CONGRESS,

JOHN HANCOCK, PRESIDENT.

ATTEST.
CHARLES THOMSON, SECRETARY.

PHILADELPHIA: PRINTED BY JOHN DUNLAP.

"THE DECLARATION OF INDEPENDENCE"

5

The Declaration of Independence

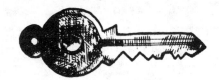

KEY WORDS

pursuit — The search for something.
The dog was in *pursuit* of the cat.

document — An important paper that tells about an agreement or something to be noticed.
Tom got his citizenship *document* from the judge.

approve — To make something official by agreeing to it.
The court must *approve* the decision.

Let us take another trip in our time machine. This is what you see if you go back to the time when the Declaration of Independence was signed.

The Declaration of Independence is written and signed during the Revolutionary War.

It is dangerous for the men who sign the document. They will be hanged if England wins the war.

Thomas Jefferson writes most of the Declaration of Independence.

What is the Declaration of Independence?

The Declaration of Independence is a list of reasons for breaking away from England. It is a statement of protest.

The Declaration of Independence is *not* a constitution. Remember — a *constitution* is a plan for a new government.

We celebrate our country's birthday on July 4, 1776. This is the date on which the Declaration of Independence is announced by the signers.

Ideas in the Declaration of Independence

Many important ideas are listed in the Declaration of Independence. These are:

All people are created equal.

We are all born with these rights:

> Life.
>
> Liberty.
>
> Pursuit of Happiness.

Let us look at the meaning of these rights.

All people are created equal. This means that we all have *equal value* as human beings whether we are rich or poor.

We deserve *Life* because as humans we must respect the value of everybody's life.

Liberty means freedom. We are free to do what we want — as long as it does not hurt other people.

Pursuit of Happiness means that we all may *search for* or "chase" happiness. Nobody can promise us that we will be happy.

The brave and brilliant men who write this Declaration give us one of the most famous documents of liberty in all of the world. It sets new ideas for individual freedom. Many countries all over the world copied these ideas.

CASE 3

The Declaration of Independence

PROBLEM:

The rebels want to write their beliefs in freedom in a noble document.

BACKGROUND:

When the war with England starts, some of the colonists want to tell the world their side.

SIGNING OF DECLARATION OF INDEPENDENCE

Choose the right word or words for each blank.

Declaration of Independence   ideas   rebel

SOLUTIONS:

The leaders of the _____ colonists write their _____

of freedom and human liberty in the _____

_____ _____ .

CHAPTER 5

What Did You Learn?

ONE: VOCABULARY

1. Match these words with their meanings:

Fill in the correct letter.

_____ 1. The search for something   A. document

_____ 2. An important paper   B. approve

_____ 3. To make something official   C. pursuit
             by agreeing to it

2. Read each sentence. Write the beginning letter that gives the **underlined word** meaning.

1. A constitution is a _____<u>lan</u> for government.   [<u>p</u>, <u>s</u>]

2. We celebrate our country's _____<u>irthday</u> on July 4.   [<u>t</u>, <u>b</u>]

3. All people are _____<u>reated</u> equal.   [<u>c</u>, <u>p</u>]

TWO: UNDERSTANDING THE FACTS

1. Fill in the right words.

1. The Declaration of Independence was announced on _____.

       A. July 4, 1776   C. October 17, 1781
       B. May 12, 1976   D. November 30, 1981

2. _____ wrote most of the Declaration of Independence.

       A. George Washington   C. Christopher Columbus
       B. King George   D. Thomas Jefferson

2. True or False?

Circle T or F:

1. It was dangerous for the men who signed the Declaration of Independence.   T F
2. The Declaration of Independence was our first constitution.   T F
3. King George liked the Declaration of Independence.   T F
4. The Declaration of Independence promises us that we will be happy.   T F
5. The ideas in the Declaration of Independence were copied by other countries.   T F

3. A Writing Project:

What are the three main ideas in the Declaration of Independence?

_____

_____

_____

_____

_____

_____

_____

_____

THREE: LEARNING THE LANGUAGE

Change each question into a statement.

Example: QUESTION — Was it dangerous for the men to sign the Declaration of Independence?

STATEMENT — It was dangerous for the men to sign the Declaration of Independence.

1. QUESTION — Was Thomas Jefferson the writer of the Declaration of Independence?

   STATEMENT — _____

2. QUESTION — Is the Declaration of Independence a statement of protest?

   STATEMENT — _____

3. QUESTION — Are all people created equal?

   STATEMENT — _____

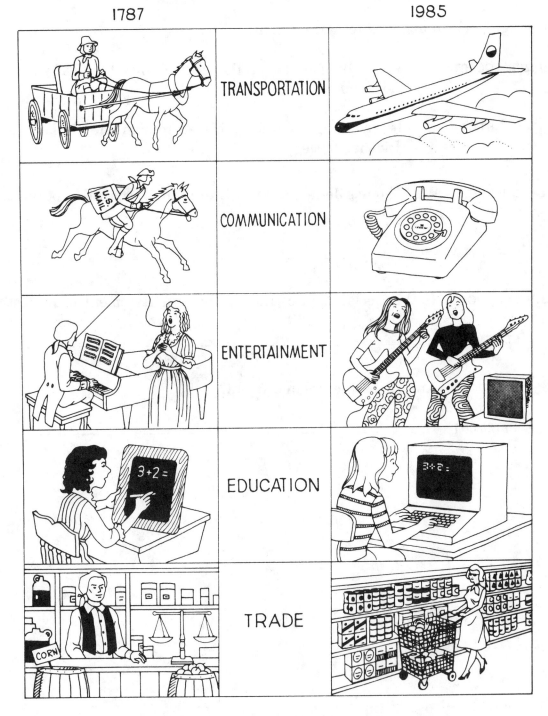

1787/1985 LAWS TO COVER THE PRESENT AND FUTURE

6

The Articles of Confederation
Our First Constitution

KEY WORDS

militia — A military group that protects the citizens of a state. (Like the national guard of today).
Each state has a *militia*.

foreign — Any country besides our own.
This car came from a *foreign* land.

Articles of Confederation — Our first constitution.
The *Articles of Confederation* did not work well because they made the national government too weak.

revise — To change something.
The President wants to *revise* the law.

independence — Freedom.
Some of the colonists wanted *independence* from England.

convention — A gathering of people.
The delegates went to the *convention*.

Our next stop on the time machine takes us to the time our country is born.

Thirteen new states

After we win our independence from England, most of the people in the thirteen new states are afraid to have a leader who is too strong. This is because of their hard times with King George III.

It is also why the constitution that they write sets up thirteen *independent* states. These states are almost like separate countries. This is our first constitution. It is called the Articles of Confederation.

Why the new government does not work

The main reason the new government does not work is that the Articles of Confederation give the states almost all of the power.

Each state has a different kind of money.

The country has few real powers and can only *ask* each state for money. The states do not want to spend money that they do not have to.

States can tax goods coming from other states.

There is no real United States army. Instead each state has its own militia.

The new United States of America has trouble dealing with other countries because it is so divided.

The government needs a change

After some years it is clear that the government is not working well. Most people know that they have to change the government. So many of the country's leaders meet to change the Articles of Confederation. They find out that the Articles are so poor that they cannot be fixed. They decide that it is better to write a whole new constitution.

CASE 4

Our First Constitution

PROBLEM:
The new country needs a government.

BACKGROUND:
Now that the United States is an independent country, they need a constitution to tell how the government should be set up.

Choose the right word or words for each blank.

Constitution   Articles of Confederation

SOLUTIONS:

The _____ _____ _____ are written and approved

as our first _____.

CASE 5

The Articles of Confederation Do Not Work

PROBLEM:

The national government is too weak under the ARTICLES OF CONFEDERATION.

BACKGROUND:

The citizens of the new government are afraid to give too much power to the national government. This is because they had too much trouble with King George III. That is why they give the states most of the power under the ARTICLES OF CONFEDERATION.

THE NATIONAL GOVERNMENT WAS TOO WEAK UNDER THE ARTICLES OF CONFEDERATION

Choose the right word or words for each blank.

      Articles of Confederation   Constitution   improve

SOLUTIONS:

A convention is held to _____ the _____ _____

_____. But they were so bad that it is easier to write a

whole new _____.

CHAPTER 6

What Did You Learn?

ONE: VOCABULARY

Write a sentence using each key word.

militia	revise
foreign	independence
Articles of Confederation	convention

1. _____

   _____

2. _____

   _____

3. _____

   _____

4. _____

   _____

5. _____

   _____

6. _____

   _____

TWO: UNDERSTANDING THE FACTS

1. Fill in the right letter.

1. The Articles of

   Confederation _____
   - A. were a big success.
   - B. became our first constitution.
   - C. were written by King George.

2. The Articles of Confederation

   did not work because _____
   - A. they gave the English too much trading power.
   - B. they let the states have most of the power.
   - C. the states had to pay too much tax to the national government.

3. When the Articles of

   Confederation did not

   work _____
   - A. most people knew that the government needed a change.
   - B. each state lost its militia.
   - C. citizens had to give soldiers shelter.

4. An independent

   country _____
   - A. is a colony of another country.
   - B. is free to run its own government.
   - C. must trade with England.

2. True or False?

Circle T or F:

1. The Articles of Confederation let each state have a different kind of money.   T   F
2. The country could collect taxes from each state even if the state did not want to pay.   T   F
3. Each state had its own army under the Articles of Confederation.   T   F
4. The Articles of Confederation made it easy for the United States to deal with other countries. T   F

THREE: LEARNING THE LANGUAGE

Prefixes. A Prefix is a syllable (part of a word) that is put at the beginning to change the word's meaning.

> *Example:* un = not

Use the Prefix "un" before each word to change its meaning. Then use it in a sentence.

> *Example:* un + known = unknown.

The new world was UNKNOWN before Columbus discovered it.

1. _____ + able = _____.

   England was _____ to win the Revolutionary War.

2. _____ + friendly = _____.

   The English and the colonists became _____.

3. _____ + kind = _____.

   King George was _____ to the colonists.

OUR CONSTITUTION IS BORN

7

Our Constitution Is Born

KEY WORDS

delegate — A person elected or chosen to go to a convention.
Jim was a *delegate* to the convention.

legislative — The part of the government that makes laws.
Congress is the *legislative* branch of our government.

executive — The branch of government that carries out the laws.
The President is the head of the *executive* branch of government.

judicial — The part of government that runs the court system.
It also decides if laws are fair.
Laws are made clear by the *judicial* branch of government.

federal — A government in which the power is shared by the national government and the states. The national government is stronger than the state government.
We have a *federal* government.

compromise — A case where two sides disagree. Each side gives up something so that both sides will get something more important.
A labor union wants a $2 per hour pay raise for its members. The company only wants to give them a $1 per hour raise. They *compromise* by both sides agreeing on a $1.50 per hour raise in pay.

representative — A person who is elected to look after other people's interests.
A member of the House of Representatives.
William Jones is the *representative* from my part of the state.

senator — A person who is elected to the United States Senate.
A *senator* votes to make laws.

If you go back in time to be at the Constitutional Convention, here is what you find.

The convention meets

The convention to write the new Constitution meets in May, 1787. They meet in the hot city of Philadelphia. They finish in September, 1787. It takes several months to write the Constitution because the delegates do not agree on everything.

Three branches of Government

The delegates finally agree on three branches for the new government. Remember — this is so that no one part of the government has all of the power — as King George III had.

These are the three branches:

Legislative
Executive
Judicial

The LEGISLATIVE branch (Congress) makes the laws.

Note: Congress is the Senate and the House of Representatives.

The EXECUTIVE branch (President) carries out or enforces the laws.

The JUDICIAL branch (courts) runs the court system. This branch also decides on the fairness of the laws.

The Constitution creates a national government which shares powers with the state governments. This is like a partnership between the state governments and the national government.

This kind of government is called a FEDERAL government. It is much stronger than the government under the Articles of Confederation. Remember — the Articles were too weak and did not work.

Political parties

Some leaders are still afraid of getting too strong a government. This is really the beginning of political parties in this country.

Parties are made up of people who think alike on how the government should be run. The people who want the new Constitution are called "Federalists." Those who are against it call themselves "Antifederalists."

What is a compromise?

When people work together and do not agree, they must COMPROMISE. A compromise is a way for each person to give a little so that they both get what they want. What if you want to go to a baseball game but your friend wants to go to the movies? You can both go to the baseball game today and agree to go to the movies tomorrow.

Here is a *compromise* that is made at the Convention. The smaller states want each state to have the same number of representatives in the new Congress (the people who make laws). These small states say that all thirteen states should be equal in power in the new government. They are all equal partners in the new government.

But the larger states say that they should have more power in the new Congress because they have more people.

Why Congress has two parts

After a while the leaders compromise. They make two parts (or "houses") of the Congress.

One part, the Senate, has two senators from each state. It does not matter how many people live in that state. *This part "favors" the small states because they have as much power as the larger states.*

However, in the House of Representatives, each state's power is based on how many people live in the state. *The larger states like this because they have more power. They have more votes in the House of Representatives.*

49

The new Constitution

The new Constitution is so well made that we still use it after two hundred years. It is written in 1787, but it is still good today.

Try to pretend that you live when the Constitution was written. You have no radio, television, telephones, cars, airplanes, electronic calculators, computers, computer games, movies, record players, or electricity. Your clothes are made only of cotton, wool, or silk. It takes days to travel short distances. You might live near a small village. You probably live on a farm since most people farm for a living.

Why the Constitution still works today

We will see later why Congress can pass laws on modern things that did not exist when the Constitution was written. This is because of a part of the Constitution called the "elastic clause."

HINT — Elastic Stretches! . . . More about this later!

CASE 6

The President Cannot Do Everything!

PROBLEM:

The colonists did not want the President to have all of the power.

BACKGROUND:

The colonists are afraid to make the President (executive) too strong because of their hard time under the English king.

THE PRESIDENT CANNOT DO EVERYTHING

Choose the right word for each blank.

        powers   government   judicial

SOLUTION:

Three branches of _____ are set up under the new

Constitution — legislative, executive, and _____. The

_____ are divided among these three branches.

CASE 7

Birth of the House of Representatives and the Senate

PROBLEM:
The smaller states want all of the states to have equal power in the legislative branch of the new government.

BACKGROUND:
The smaller states feel that each state should be equal in the new government. The larger states claim that the states with the most people should have more representatives.

Choose the right word for each blank.

more   senators   compromise

SOLUTIONS:

They agree on a _____. The new Congress has two houses.

The smaller states like the Senate better. This is because each state, big or

small, has two _____.

The larger states like the House of Representatives better because larger

states have _____ representatives than smaller states.

Now both the smaller and larger states can share power. Both get what they want.

Sometimes a _____ is a good way for two sides to agree.

> FREE MINIFACT
> The word "state" really meant country at the
> time the Constitution was born.

CHAPTER 7

What Did You Learn?

ONE: VOCABULARY

1. Read each sentence. Write the key word which best completes the meaning of the sentence.

delegate   federal
legislative   compromise
executive   representative
judicial   senator

1. George Washington was a _____ to the convention.   [delegate, dealer]

2. Congress is the _____ branch of our federal government.   [legislative, long]

3. The _____ branch of government carries out the laws.   [equal, executive]

4. The _____ branch of government runs the court system.   [joyful, judicial]

5. We have a _____ government.   [foreign, federal]

6. A good way to settle an argument

   is to _____.   [complain, compromise]

7. A _____ is elected to look after other people's interests.   [representative, rancher]

8. A _____ is elected to the United States Senate.   [senator, seller]

2. Match these words.

Fill in the right letter.

1. convention ___   A. interprets the laws.

2. delegates ___   B. member of the Senate.

3. legislative ___   C. meeting.

4. executive ___   D. members of a convention.

5. judicial ___   E. makes the laws.

6. federal ___   F. the President's branch of government.

7. senator ___   G. our national government.

TWO: UNDERSTANDING THE FACTS

1. Fill in the right letter.

1. It took several months to write the new Constitution because _____.

     A. the delegates did not agree on everything.
     B. the cool weather in Philadelphia made the delegates want to stay there longer.
     C. the English did not want to help.

2. The new Constitution set up these three branches: _____.

     A. federal, state, and local.
     B. legislative, executive, and judicial.
     C. New York, New Jersey, Virginia.

3. A compromise is _____.

     A. a type of agreement.
     B. an argument.
     C. a type of tax.

4. Congress has two parts because _____.

        A. the Americans wanted to copy the English government.
        B. this satisfied both large and small states in a famous compromise.
        C. there was an odd number of states in the country.

2. True or False?

Circle T or F:

1. The executive branch of government carries out or enforces the laws.	T F
2. The legislative branch runs the court system.	T F
3. In a federal government power is shared by the national and state governments.	T F
4. Our Constitution was so well written that it is still good after almost 200 years.	T F
5. Political parties are made up of people who think alike on how the country should work.	T F

3. Writing Project:

Write a short paragraph telling about the three branches of government.

_____

_____

_____

_____

_____

_____

THREE: LEARNING THE LANGUAGE

Word Order

Unscramble these sentences. Each sentence begins with a capital letter. End each sentence with a period.

Example: door the locked was

The door was locked.

1. government has our three branches

   Our _____

2. laws President out the carries

   The _____

3. Congress of two we have houses

   We _____

4. today Constitution works still our

   Our _____

5. have we a government federal

   We _____

8

How the Constitution Is Set Up

KEY WORDS

preamble — The statement that tells us the purpose of the constitution.
   It is before the main part of the Constitution.
   The president of the convention read the *preamble* to the delegates.

domestic tranquility — Peace at home or in our country.
   The police chief makes sure that there is *domestic tranquility* in the town.

Union — Another word for the United States.
   This word was used more when our country was young.
   The Civil War was fought to save the *Union*.

posterity — The future.
   A fund of money was set up for *posterity*.

The writers of the Constitution wrote it in a form that makes sense. They wrote it like an outline.

   The Constitution begins with a message that tells the purpose of the Constitution. This message is called the *Preamble* to the Constitution.

The Preamble

We the people of the United States, in order to form a more perfect Union, establish justice, insure domestic tranquility, provide for the common defense, promote the general welfare, and secure the blessings of liberty to ourselves and our posterity, do ordain and establish this Constitution for the United States of America.

This preamble tells us that the writers of the Constitution want to make a stronger, more perfect government. They also want one that will keep the peace and be fair to everyone. The new Constitution gives us liberty and also saves it for future citizens of our country.

The articles

The main part of the Constitution is also written in a clear way. The important subjects are called *articles*.

These "articles" are like chapters in a book. For example, ARTICLE I is about the LEGISLATIVE branch (Congress). ARTICLE II tells us about the EXECUTIVE branch (President). The JUDICIAL branch is in ARTICLE III.

How to remember the first three articles

Sometimes it helps to remember facts if you use a word clue. If you think of the nonsense word "LEJ," you can remember the first three articles in order.

> ARTICLE I ——— L for "Legislative."
>
> ARTICLE II —— E for "Executive."
>
> ARTICLE III — J for "Judicial."

So if you want to find out how old a representative must be, you would find it in Article I.

The other four articles

Since there are only seven articles in the Constitution, you already know what is in three out of the seven articles (3/7).

The other articles are:

> ARTICLE IV —— Relations Between the National and State Governments.
>
> ARTICLE V ——— How to Make Changes in the Constitution.
>
> ARTICLE VI —— Odds and Ends (miscellaneous).
>
> ARTICLE VII — How the New Constitution is to Be Approved.

CASE 8

Plan of the New Constitution

PROBLEM:

The writers of the Constitution want to write it in a way that makes sense.

BACKGROUND:

The people who write the Constitution want it to be set up in good form.

Choose the right word for each blank.

      preamble   chapter

SOLUTIONS:

A _____ is written in front of the Constitution to explain

its purpose. The rest of the Constitution is arranged in "articles." Each article is

like a _____ in a book because it tells about one subject. For example,
Article II tells about the President.

CHAPTER 8

What Did You Learn?

ONE: VOCABULARY

1. Use the key words to complete each sentence.

preamble   union

domestic tranquility   posterity

1. _____ means the future.

2. Peace in the country is called _____ _____ .

3. The _____ tells us the purpose of a Constitution.

4. _____ is another word for the United States.

2. Crossword. Fill in the blanks with the following words. Use the definitions to help you.

domestic   union

plan   posterity

articles   preamble

DEFINITIONS

Across

1. This tells us the purpose of the Constitution.
2. _____ in the Constitution are like chapters in a book.
3. Another word for the United States.

Down

1. The future.
4. _____ tranquility means peace in the country.
5. The Constitution is a _____ for the federal government.

TWO: UNDERSTANDING THE FACTS

1. Fill in the right word.

1. The writers of the Constitution wrote it in the form of an _____.

    A. outline   C. atlas

    B. opera   D. independence

2. The preamble tells the _____ of the Constitution.

    A. list   C. date

    B. purpose   D. dangers

3. The Constitution is written in a clear way because the important subjects

   are arranged in _____.

    A. articles   C. verses

    B. semesters   D. preambles

4. Articles I is about the _____ branch.

    A. legislative   C. tree

    B. citizenship   D. freedom

2. True or False?

Circle T or F:

1. The writers of the Constitution wanted to make
   a better government.   T   F
2. The President is mentioned in Article II.   T   F
3. If you want to find out what the Senate does,
   you look in Article I.   T   F
4. Article I also tells us what the courts do.   T   F

THREE: LEARNING THE LANGUAGE

Synonyms. A synonym is a word that means almost the same as another word.

Example: happy   glad

Circle the synonym for each word.

Example:	hot	(warm)	hard	cold
1.	fast	slow	sad	quick
2.	big	round	tiny	large
3.	late	tardy	early	fast
4.	automobile	desk	train	car
5.	easy	hard	simple	flat

9

The Bill of Rights

KEY WORDS

amendment — Something that is added. A change in the Constitution.
Many people want to add an *amendment* to the Constitution that gives women equal rights.

freedom — When you can decide your own goals and what you do. Liberty.
The girl had the *freedom* to go out at night.

responsibility — Something that you should do.
We have a *responsibility* for what we do.

jury — A group of ordinary citizens who decide who is telling the truth in a court case.
A jury usually has twelve people.
The *jury* decided that Henry was not guilty because there were not enough facts against him.

assemble — When a group of people meet in one place.
They *assemble* to decide what to do.

slander — A lie about somebody that is spoken.
The president of the bank sued John for *slander* because John's lies about him made people take their money out of his bank.

libel — A lie that is written about somebody.
The newspaper printed a false story. They were accused of *libel*.

trial — A case or lawsuit to see if somebody is guilty of a crime.
The woman had a *trial* to see if she was guilty of slander.

Another compromise

Do you still remember what the word "compromise" means? A compromise is when each side gives up something that it wants to get some of what they want.

Here is another compromise. Let us return to the Constitution Convention. Many people are afraid that the new Constitution does not protect the people's rights. *Federalists* are people who want the new Constitution badly. They must add promises for the peoples' rights to get enough votes to get the new Constitution.

These promises are called the *Bill of Rights*.

Amendments

An *amendment* changes or adds something to the Constitution. The word *amendment* means change.

The first ten amendments to the Constitution are called the *Bill of Rights*. The Bill of Rights is the part of the Constitution that protects our rights.

The Bill of Rights are added soon after the main part of the Constitution. This makes many people think of the Bill of Rights as part of the original Constitution.

Our freedom

Many of the freedoms that we take for granted are in the Bill of Rights. Some of the most important of these are:
Freedom of Speech.
Freedom of Religion.
Freedom of the Press.
Freedom from Unreasonable Search and Seizure.

The Right to Peacefully Meet.

The Right to a Trial by Jury.

The Right to a Free and Speedy Trial.

These rights are the main difference between a free country and a dictatorship. England did not give the colonists most of these rights.

Limits on our rights

Almost all of these rights have limits to them. For example, my freedom of speech does not let me start a riot in a movie theater by yelling "FIRE" when there is none. I cannot sing in front of your house late at night. My freedom stops as soon as I interfere with someone else's freedom. I also cannot call the president of a bank a "crook" just because I am angry with him. If I cause his bank to lose money because of my lies, the bank president can sue me for *slander*.

Freedom of the Press means that our newspapers may print whatever is true and in good taste. Our newspapers are free to print stories about our government. They can print anything about the President, governor, or mayor that is true.

But a newspaper cannot print lies on purpose. If these lies hurt a person's reputation, that person might sue for *libel*.

CASE 9

The Bill of Rights

PROBLEM:

Many of the leaders will not sign or approve of the new Constitution unless it promises certain rights to the people.

BACKGROUND:

Some colonists do not trust the stronger federal government. They want to make sure that the citizens have important rights.

Freedom
of
Speech

Freedom
of
Press

Freedom of Religion

THE BILL OF RIGHTS

Choose the right word for each blank.

Rights   amendments   Constitution

SOLUTION:

A set of ten _____ is added to the _____.

These amendments are called the Bill of _____. They promise many rights that make our country great.

67

CASE 10

Our Rights Do Not Let Us Hurt Other People

PROBLEM:

People might think that the freedoms mentioned in the Bill of Rights give them the right to do whatever they want.

BACKGROUND:

For example, a person might say something untrue about another person and hurt the other person's reputation.

OUR RIGHTS DO NOT LET US HURT OTHER PEOPLE

Choose the right word for each blank.

takes away   freedom

SOLUTION:

The Supreme Court ruled that one person's _____ ends when he

or she _____ _____ another person's freedom.

FREE MINIFACT

Amendments are the "formal" way to change the Constitution. Later we will see that the meaning of the Constitution changes daily through the court system.

CHAPTER 9

What Did You Learn?

ONE: VOCABULARY

1. Use the key words to complete the paragraphs.

responsibility	jury
libel	trial

Mr. Jones sued the newspaper for _____ because he said that

the newspaper printed a lie about him. There was a _____ to see

if the newspaper was guilty. A _____ of twelve people decided

that the newspaper was not guilty. The jury has the _____ to
find out who is telling the truth.

assemble	amendment
freedom	

The delegates _____d to talk about adding an

_____ to the Constitution. They talked about the

_____s in the Bill of Rights.

2. Read each sentence. Write the beginning letter that gives the underlined word meaning.

1.   The Bill of _____ights gives us many freedoms.   [S, R]

2.   A _____ompromise is a way to settle an argument.   [b, c]

3.   One important freedom that we have is freedom of the ____ress.   [t, p]

4.   _____lander is a lie about someone that is spoken.   [B, S]

69

TWO: UNDERSTANDING THE FACTS

1. Fill in the right letter.

   1. The Bill of Rights _____

       A. was written by the King of England.
       B. promises us many of our rights.
       C. gives us the right to do anything we want.

   2. Federalists were _____

       A. people who wanted the new Constitution.
       B. a baseball team.
       C. people who wanted to keep the Articles of Confederation.

   3. If we are in trouble with the law and have to go to court we have the right to

   _____

       A. stay away from court.
       B. have a trial by jury.
       C. choose a good judge to hear the case.

   4. An amendment is _____

       A. something that is added to the Constitution.
       B. a group of people who decide the truth in a case.
       C. a compromise.

2. True or False?

Circle T or F:

1. Everybody at the Constitution Convention agreed on everything.	T F
2. Our right of free speech lets us say whatever we want.	T F
3. The Bill of Rights were added soon after the delegates wrote the Constitution.	T F
4. Our newspapers can give their opinions on our leaders.	T F
5. Many leaders did not trust the new federal government so they wanted the Bill of Rights.	T F

THREE: LEARNING THE LANGUAGE

Antonyms. An antonym is a word that means the opposite of another word.

Example: hot   cold

Circle the antonym for each word.

Example: good   kind   (bad)   tall

   1. in   over   under   out

   2. fast   funny   slow   quick

   3. up   down   far   high

   4. happy   cheerful   nice   sad

   5. open   shut   wide   deep

10

Article I
The Legislative Branch

KEY WORDS

Capitol — The dome-shaped building in which Congress meets. A building in which a legislature meets.
The *Capitol* is one of the most famous buildings in Washington, D.C.

house — The Senate or the House of Representatives.
These are the two *houses* in Congress.

ambassador — A person who speaks for a country in another country.
The Mexican *ambassador* spoke to the President of the United States about an agreement between their two countries.

cabinet member — A person who is in charge of one of the departments in the executive part of government. This person reports directly to the President.
The Secretary of State is a *cabinet member*.

treaty — An agreement between countries.
The United States signed a *treaty* with China.

72

enumerated powers — Things Congress can do that are clearly written in the Constitution.

The power to coin money is an *enumerated power* because it says so in the Constitution.

elastic clause — The section of the Constitution that gives Congress the power to make laws on things that are not listed in the Constitution. It says that Congress can make laws on things that are "necessary and proper." It has the nickname "elastic" because elastic stretches.

Congress can pass laws on space travel because of the *elastic clause.*

The first article

The first article of the Constitution is about *Congress.* Congress is the *legislative* branch of the government. Its main job is to pass laws for our country.

What Congress does

Passing Laws

This is the main duty that the Constitution gives to Congress. Both houses are involved because a bill cannot become a law unless it passes both "houses" of Congress.

Other Powers of Congress (enumerated powers)

These are a few of the enumerated (listed) powers of Congress:

Congress has taxing powers.

It can borrow money and make rules about trade with other countries.

Congress makes rules about how people can become citizens.

Congress prints and coins our money.

It also has the power to declare war if the United States is attacked by an enemy.

What Is the Elastic Clause?

The people who wrote the Constitution were very wise. At the end of Article I, they wrote that Congress can make all laws that are necessary and proper to run the government.

This is the ELASTIC CLAUSE. It has the nickname of "elastic clause" because elastic stretches.

The elastic clause stretches the power of Congress to make laws on new things. These are not heard of when the Constitution is written.

If the law is "necessary and proper," then Congress can pass it. We shall see later that the court system is the final "umpire" on what is really necessary and proper.

Remember — the powers that are actually *written down* in the Constitution are *enumerated powers*. Congress takes some powers because of changes or new inventions. The elastic clause gives Congress these powers.

What Congress cannot do

Here are some of the things that the Constitution says that Congress may *not* do.

Congress may *not:*

>Hold a person in prison illegally.
>
>Pass a law that only punishes one person or one group.
>
>Pass a law that punishes people for something they did before the law was passed.

Let us say that the city puts a NO PARKING sign in front of my house *today.* I have been parking there for years. There was no sign during that time. They cannot ticket me because I parked there yesterday.

Grant titles of nobility. This means that Congress cannot make certain people princes, barons, and earls.

States may not do these things:

>Make a treaty with a foreign country.
>
>Create their own money system.
>
>Examine goods coming in or out of each state.

The Two Houses of Congress

Congress has two "houses" called the House of Representatives and the Senate. The term "house" means branches — not buildings. Both "houses" really are in the same building — the Capitol Building.

The House of Representatives

Duties

>Their main job is to pass laws with the Senate.
>
>They also play a part in removing a President or federal judge who does not behave well.

The House of Representatives has 435 members. There is one member for about 500,000 persons in a state.

States with more people have more representatives than smaller states.

Each representative has a district that he or she represents.

Representatives receive a yearly salary.

Representatives keep their jobs for two years. They may run again as many times as they want.

Representatives Must:
Be at least twenty-five years old.

Be citizens for at least seven years.

Live in the district they represent.

The Senate

Duties
The Senate's main job is to pass laws with the House of Representatives. The Senate must agree to the President's choices for these jobs before the people can work in the jobs:

> *Cabinet members* (people who help the President), *ambassadors* (people who go to other countries to represent our government), and *federal judges*.

Senators help to make new amendments (changes in the Constitution). They also play a part in firing a President or federal judge who does not behave well.

Important Facts
Each state, big or little, has two senators.

We have 50 states in the country, so there are 100 members in the Senate.

The Senate is the house that favors the smaller states because they have the same number of people in the Senate (2) as the larger states.

A senator has a yearly salary.

Senators keep their jobs for six years. They may run for as many terms as they want.

Senators Must:
Live in the state they represent, be at least 30 years old, and be a citizen for at least nine years.

CASE 11

Elastic Clause

PROBLEM:

Congress must be able to make laws on things that are not listed in the Constitution.

BACKGROUND:

The writers of the Constitution knew that they could not possibly list everything that the new government must do.

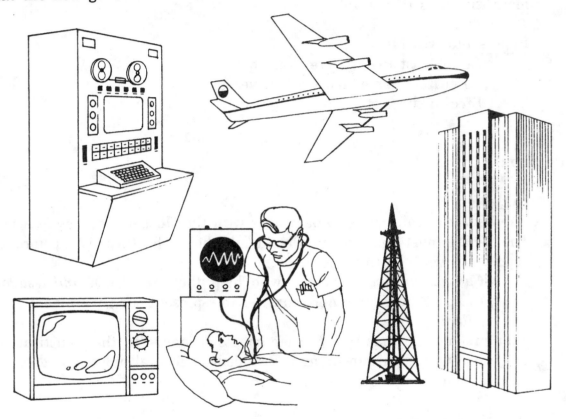

THE ELASTIC CLAUSE LET CONGRESS PASS LAWS ON NEW THINGS

Choose the right word for each blank.

proper   listed   Constitution

SOLUTION:

The writers of the _____ wisely included words (elastic clause) that say that Congress shall have the power to make all

laws that are necessary and _____. This lets Congress pass laws on

important things that are not _____ in the Constitution.

76

CASE 12

"No No's" for the Federal Government

PROBLEM:

There are some powers that the people wanted to keep away from the new government.

BACKGROUND:

The citizens of the new country wanted to make sure that the new government would let them keep their freedoms.

"NO NO'S" FOR THE FEDERAL GOVERNMENT

Choose the right word for each blank.

    prison   punishes   person

SOLUTION:

The Constitution lists things that the government cannot do.

Examples: The government cannot:

1. Hold a person in _____ illegally.

2. Pass a law that _____ only one _____ or group.

3. Grant titles of nobility, (Dukes, earls, counts, etc.)

   to a _____.

CASE 13

"No No's" for the States

PROBLEM:

States might try to make agreements with foreign countries by themselves or create their own money system. This would hurt the national government.

BACKGROUND:

Under the Articles of Confederation, states were like separate countries. This made the national government weak.

STATES WERE LIKE SEPARATE COUNTRIES

Choose the right word for each blank.

       Constitution   powers

SOLUTION:

    The _____ tells some _____ that the states may not have.

CHAPTER 10

What Did You Learn?

ONE: VOCABULARY

1. Choose the key word that makes the most sense.

HINT: Look for more than one way to say the same thing.

1. Congress meets in a dome-shape building. The _____ is one of the prettiest buildings in Washington, D.C.
   - A. Capitol
   - B. document
   - C. United States
   - D. amendment

2. Congress has two parts. They are the Senate and the _____ of Representatives.
   - A. election
   - B. House
   - C. room
   - D. building

3. Mr. Martinez went to Mexico to explain our country's ideas. He is an

   _____ of the United States.
   - A. aliens
   - B. enemy
   - C. ambassador
   - D. editor

4. Ms. White is in charge of the State Department. She is a _____.
   - A. cabinet member
   - B. senator
   - C. representative
   - D. mayor

5. The United States signed a trade agreement with Japan. This is called a

   _____.
   - A. newspaper
   - B. city
   - C. slander
   - D. treaty

6. The Constitution clearly says that Congress can coin money. This written

   power is an _____ power.
   - A. enumerated
   - B. able
   - C. energy
   - D. eager

7. Congress passed a law on airport safety. The _____ clause gives Congress the right to pass laws on things that are not clearly listed in the Constitution.

    A. dental   C. elastic

    B. santa   D. money

TWO: UNDERSTANDING THE FACTS

1. Fill in the right words.

1. Article _____ tells us about Congress.

    A. I   C. III

    B. II   D. IV

2. Congress is the Senate and the _____.

    A. White House   C. Supreme Court

    B. President   D. House of Representatives

3. The _____ lets Congress pass laws on things not mentioned in the Constitution.

    A. elastic clause   C. Fifth Amendment

    B. President   D. taxing power

4. The Senate and the House of Representatives are the two houses of

    _____.

    A. the President   C. the court system

    B. Congress   D. patents

5. The Senate and the House of Representatives have their offices in the

    _____ Building.

    A. Capitol   C. White House

    B. court   D. Article

2. True or False?

Circle T or F:

1. Cabinet members work for senators.   T F
2. We have royalty in the United States.   T F
3. The ENUMERATED POWERS are listed in the Constitution.   T F

4. Congress has the power to make rules
   about how people become citizens.   T F
5. Congress can pass a law that punishes
   someone for doing something
   before the law was passed.   T F
6. The Senate has more members than the House
   of Representatives.   T F
7. Each state has two senators.   T F
8. A bill can become a law if only the Senate
   votes for it.   T F
9. The people in the House of
   Representatives are picked
   by the President.   T F
10. The main job of Congress is passing laws.   T F

THREE: LEARNING THE LANGUAGE

Unscramble these sentences: Each sentence begins with a capital letter. End each sentence with a period.

Example: are senators 100 there

        There are 100 senators.

1. taxing powers has Congress

   _____

2. make money states may not own their

   _____

3. two parts Congress has

   _____

4. senators each two has state

   _____

5. laws passes Congress

   _____

The White House after the 1952 restoration. Above: The South Portico with the new balcony. Below: The North Portico and main entrance.

11

Article II
The Executive Branch

KEY WORDS

Commander-in-Chief — The person at the highest level of leadership.
The President is *Commander-in-Chief* of the armed forces.

enforce — To see that something is "carried out."
The President's job is to *enforce* laws that Congress passes.

veto — A single vote against a bill that stops the bill from passing.
Presidents *veto* bills that they do not want to become laws.

Article II
Article II tells us about the executive branch of the federal government. The President is the leader of the executive branch. So, Article II has everything that the *main part* of the Constitution says about the President.

    The Constitution has some amendments about the President. These amendments were written after the main part of the Constitution.

Duties of the President

Enforcing the Country's Laws

The President's main job under the Constitution is to enforce the laws that are created by Congress.

This means that the President sees that the laws are followed.

Signing Bills to Make Laws

If the President signs a bill after it passes both houses of Congress, it becomes a law. But if the President does not want the bill to become a law, the President can veto it by refusing to sign it.

This time, at least 2/3 of the members of both houses must vote for the bill before it can be a law.

Commander-in-Chief of the Armed Forces

The President is the Commander-in-Chief of all of the armed forces. (The armed forces are the army, navy, air force, and marines.) The President is higher in rank than any general or admiral. This is true even if the President was never in the armed forces. This makes sure that we always have a civilian government instead of a military one. But all of our recent Presidents were in the armed forces.

Leader of Their Party

Presidents hold the highest political job in the United States. So they are the head of their party.

Parties are not even mentioned in the Constitution. Think of parties as *teams*. They started because everybody did not agree on the ideas of government.

Our country has a strong two-party system — Democrats and Republicans. Each party tries to get votes from the voters.

Many people vote a "straight ticket." This means that they always vote for a person of their party. So, a Democrat would vote for all of the Democrats who are running in the election. A Republican voter would vote for all of the Republicans on the ballot.

"Independent voters" vote for each office separately. These people feel that no party has all of the good people. They look at each candidate carefully before they vote.

Making Treaties

Treaties are agreements signed by the United States and another country. These treaties may be about many subjects. They may be about trade, peace, or defense.

After the President signs a treaty, the SENATE must approve it before the treaty is valid.

Choosing Federal Judges

The President chooses all of the federal judges. The Senate must approve of the President's choices.

A President Must:

Be thirty-five years old or older.

Be born in the United States and live in this country for at least 14 years.

Only have two terms of four years. This was not always true. Article II of the Constitution does not tell how many years a President may serve.

The 22nd Amendment made this a part of the Constitution.

The requirements are the same for the Vice President. The Vice President might become President.

CHAPTER 11

What Did You Learn?

ONE: VOCABULARY

1. Match these words with their meanings.

    _____ 1. A single vote against a bill
                  that stops the bill.   A. Commander-in-Chief

    _____ 2. The person at the highest level. B. enforce

    _____ 3. To see that something is
                  carried out.   C. veto

2. Can you unscramble these words?

    1. EPPOVAR _____   To show that you like something.

    2. FCENREO _____   To see that a law is "carried out."

    3. TOVE _____   A single vote against a bill that stops it
                                 from becoming a law.

                              Hints
          enforce   veto   approve

TWO: UNDERSTANDING THE FACTS

1. Fill in the right word.

    1. Article II tells us about the _____ branch of government.

            A. executive   C. legislative
            B. judicial   D. local

    2. The President is the _____ of the Executive branch.

            A. sponsor   C. helper
            B. leader   D. soldier

86

3. Congress passes _____ that it wants to be laws.

    A. bills   C. days

    B. contracts   D. memos

4. After Congress passes a bill, the President _____ it if he or she wants it to be a law.

    A. notes   C. files

    B. signs   D. rejects

5. The President is _____ of the armed forces.

    A. Commander-in-Chief   C. sergeant

    B. mascot   D. mayor

6. Treaties are _____ signed by the United States and another country.

    A. warnings   C. invitations

    B. agreements   D. pieces

7. The _____ chooses all of the federal judges.

    A. governor   C. House of Representatives

    B. Chief Justice   D. President

8. The President stays in office for _____ years each time he or she is elected.

    A. 7   C. 8

    B. 5   D. 4

2. True or False?

Circle T or F:

1. A bill must be passed by both houses of Congress to be a law.   T F
2. A President can pass a bill by himself.   T F
3. Members of Congress enforce the laws.   T F
4. The President can vote on a bill in the Senate.   T F
5. The United States has two main parties.   T F

3. Name five duties of the President.

1. _____

2. _____

3. _____

4. _____

5. _____

THREE: LEARNING THE LANGUAGE

A suffix is a syllable (part of a word) added to the end of a word to form another word. Sometimes it changes the meaning of a word.

Example:	**Base Word**	**Suffix**	**New Word**
	sign	+ ing	signing

Use the suffix "ing" after each word to change its meaning.

Example: break + ing = breaking

He was punished for breaking the law.

1. lead + ing = _____

The President is _____ the executive department.

2. elect + ing = _____

The country is _____ a President.

3. think + ing = _____

Congress is _____ of new ways to help people.

4. look + ing = _____

The voters are _____ carefully at each candidate.

5. pass + ing = _____

Congress is _____ new tax laws.

12

The President's Cabinet

KEY WORDS

attorney — A lawyer. One who knows about laws and can appear in court to help people.
His *attorney* helped him to win the case.

Attorney General — The cabinet member who is the head of the Justice Department.
The chief lawyer for the United States is the *Attorney General*.

interior — "Inside."
The *Secretary of the Interior* takes care of the government land "inside" of the United States. (National parks and Indian affairs.)

State Department — The President's department that deals with other countries.
The Secretary of State runs the *State Department*.

urban — Having to do with cities or crowded areas.
The *Urban Department* is the cabinet department that deals with problems of cities.

What are cabinet members?

Cabinet members are people who head the departments in the executive (President's) branch. These cabinet members advise the President and help to run these departments.

What the Constitution says about cabinet members

The Constitution does not mention the word "cabinet." It says that the President may ask for the opinions of the main officers.

George Washington started the custom of picking cabinet members. He had only four members in his cabinet. But as our government became more complicated, we needed more cabinet members.

What the cabinet members are called

The heads of these departments are called "secretaries." The only one who is not is the head of the Justice Department. This person is called the "Attorney General."

Our cabinet departments today

These are the cabinet departments that we have now:

State Department —

This department deals with other countries. AMBASSADORS are people who speak for the United States when we talk with other countries. Ambassadors work for the State Department.

Justice Department —

This department represents the United States in courts. The Attorney General is the chief lawyer in the federal government.

Defense Department —

The Defense Department deals with our armed forces. Do not forget that the President is "Commander-in-Chief" of the armed forces!

Interior Department —

The word "interior" means *inside*. So, the Secretary of Interior deals with land and natural resources *inside* our country. The Secretary of the Interior runs our National Park System and also is in charge of Indian affairs.

Labor Department—

The Labor Department deals with workers. This is an important department because so many Americans are workers.

Commerce Department—

This department deals with business. "Commerce" means *business*. So the Secretary of Commerce helps to solve problems of business and industry.

Treasury Department—

The Secretary of the Treasury manages our country's money.

Health and Human Services Department—

This cabinet member is in charge of the federal health programs. The Food and Drug Administration and Social Security are two of the main jobs of this department.

Housing and Urban Development —

"Urban" means *city*. So this department helps with problems of big cities, especially housing.

Transportation Department—

This department solves problems of transportation — land, water, and air.

Energy Department —

The Energy Department deals with energy use and development. This is an important department because oil, natural gas, and coal are so important to us.

Education Department—

The Education Department controls all of the federal programs that deal with education.

REMEMBER — *These cabinet members give the President advice. They also run their departments.*

CHAPTER 12

What Did You Learn?

ONE: VOCABULARY

1. Fill in the key word:

   attorney   State Department
   Attorney General   urban
   Interior

   1. An _____ is a lawyer.

   2. _____ has to do with cities.

   3. The _____ _____ deals with other countries.

   4. The _____ _____ is the head of the Justice Department.

   5. The Secretary of the _____ takes care of the government's land.

2. Crossword. Fill in the blanks from the following words. Use the definitions to help you.

attorney   state
cabinet   urban
interior

DEFINITIONS

Across

1. _____ members run the President's Departments.
2. The Department of _____ takes care of our national parks.

Down

3. Having to do with cities.
4. The _____ Department deals with other countries.
5. A lawyer.

TWO: UNDERSTANDING THE FACTS

1. Fill in the right words.

1. _____ are people who head the President's departments.

   A. Clerks   C. Senators
   B. Cabinet members   D. Interiors

2. The cabinet department that deals with other countries is the _____.

   A. Treasury Department   C. Commerce Department
   B. Labor Department   D. State Department

3. The _____ Department deals with air travel.

      A. Labor   C. Transportation
      B. Money   D. State

4. The Treasury Department manages our country's _____.

      A. national parks   C. labor unions
      B. money   D. army

5. This department sees that we have good food and drugs: _____.

      A. Interior   C. Treasury
      B. Defense   D. Health and Human Services

2. True or False?

Circle T or F:

1. The Labor Department's main job is to help farmers. T F
2. The Supreme Court picks the cabinet members
   for the President.   T F
3. New York City is an urban area.   T F
4. The Education Department helps schools. T F
5. The State Department takes care of state parks. T F

THREE: LEARNING THE LANGUAGE

Synonyms. A synonym is a word that means almost the same as another word.

Example: labor   work

Circle the synonym for each word.

Example: labor   jump   (work)   trust

1. commerce   business   movies   parks

2. education   drawing   learning   sleeping

3. urban   train   plane   cities

4. interior   inside   outside   under

5. lawyer   painter   attorney   doctor

13

How A President Is Elected

KEY WORDS

electoral college — A group of people who select the President by counting the electoral votes from each state.
The *electoral college* selects the President.

electors — Members of the electoral college.
The *electors* choose the President.

electoral vote — The vote by state for President and Vice President.
President Kennedy won the election because he had more *electoral votes* from the states.

popular vote — The actual vote of the people.
The number of votes from the people. This decides the winner in every election except for the President.
President Kennedy also won the *popular vote* because more Americans voted for him.

impeachment — To accuse a President of conduct so bad as to be reason to lose the job of President. The first step in removing a President. The House of Representatives does this.
President Andrew Johnson was *impeached*.

96

conviction — Being found guilty of something illegal.

This is the second step in removing a President from office. First the House of Representatives votes to impeach a President. Then the Senate must vote to *convict* the President before he or she loses the job. The Senate did not vote to *convict* President Andrew Johnson, so he remained President until the end of his term.

nominate — To choose a person for a job.

Presidents are *nominated* at their party's conventions.

political party — A group of people who agree on many things.

The Democrats and the Republicans are our two major *political parties*.

candidate — A person who is running for an office.

A person who is picked by a party to run for an office.

Tom Johnson is the Democratic Party's *candidate* for mayor.

Elections

There is a Presidential election every four years. It is held in November.

How parties choose their candidate

Each party chooses a person to run for President. This person is "nominated" by the party.

Think of each party as a team. The person who is selected is like the captain of the team.

The person who is chosen by the party is their candidate.

The candidate is chosen at the party's convention. The convention is held in July or August of the election year.

The candidate for each party runs against the other in the November election.

The Electoral College

Here is something that might surprise you! Your friends and relatives vote for many different candidates. But they *never* vote *directly* for President.

Your friends vote for "electors" who vote for the candidates. The electors are people whose job is to meet after the people vote and select the President.

These electors form the electoral college, which actually selects the candidate for President. THE ELECTORAL COLLEGE IS NOT A SCHOOL.

The President (and the Vice President) are the only candidates who are elected by the electoral college.

The popular vote

The people's vote is called the POPULAR VOTE. This is the total number of votes from the people. The *popular vote* decides who wins in all of elections *except elections for President.*

Why the electoral college was created

The writers of the Constitution were rich and educated men. They were not really like most of the people at the time. In those days, most of the people were poor farmers. They also did not have as much education as the writers of the Constitution.

The men who wrote the Constitution thought that all citizens should vote. But they were afraid to completely trust the common man to always elect a good President. So they created the ELECTORAL COLLEGE.

When someone votes for President, the candidates' names are on the ballot. But the votes are really for electors whose names are not known to the voters.

How the electors are chosen

The number of electors in each state is figured by how many people are in the state.

Each state's vote is counted separately. This means that the candidate who gets the most votes from the people in each state receives *all* of the electoral votes for that state. It is as though nobody cast a single vote for the loser. The winner in each state gets all of the "marbles."

Unfortunately, it is possible for someone to win the presidency who does not receive a majority of the people's vote.

This is why many people would like to have an amendment to the Constituiton which does away with the electoral college. These people think that the average voter *can* be trusted to vote for a good candidate. They also think that the person who gets the most votes from the people should always be President.

How a President may be fired

The Constitution tells us how to remove a President who is guilty of treason, bribery, or other bad crimes.

What is impeachment?

Many people think that if Presidents are "impeached" they lose their jobs.

Impeachment alone does not mean that the President would lose his or her job. Impeachment is only half of the process. There are two parts to the job of firing a President who does not behave well.

Impeachment and conviction
There are two steps that must happen before Presidents may be forced out of their jobs.

Here are the two steps:

Impeachment — (By the House of Representatives)
This is the first step. It always starts in the House of Representatives. The House of Representatives votes to "impeach" the President.

If most of the members of the House of Representatives do not vote against the President, that is the end of the process.

If most of them do vote to impeach the President, the President does not lose the job yet. Now the Senate must decide if the charges are true.

Conviction — (By the Senate)
The Senate hears the case only if the House of Representatives impeaches the President. The Senate never starts the process.

If the House impeaches the President, the Senate hears the evidence. The Senate's job is to decide if there is enough evidence to make the person serving as President lose the job. (The Senate is like a jury in this case.)

The Senate may vote that the facts show that the President behaved badly. Then the person serving as President would lose the job.

We had a President who was *impeached*. But he did not lose his office.

Andrew Johnson was the man who became President after Abraham Lincoln was shot. He was *impeached* by the House of Representatives. But the Senate did not vote to *convict* him.

Do not forget that the Senate must also vote against Presidents before they lose their jobs!

What Happens if the President dies or becomes very ill?
The government cannot stop if something happens to the President. If the President dies or becomes too ill to do the job, the Vice President takes over the job of President.

Then, the Vice President is President until the next election. But what if something bad happens to the Vice President?

Order of people who become President

Here is the order of people who become President in case of death or illness of the President:

1. Vice President.
2. Speaker of the House of Representatives (the leader of the House of Representatives).
3. President Pro Tempore of the Senate (the leader of the Senate).
4. Cabinet members (starting with the Secretary of State).

CASE 14

Electoral College

PROBLEM:

Many people think that the electoral college is not a fair way to elect a President since the voters do not vote directly for the President.

BACKGROUND:

The writers of the Constitution wanted the country's leaders to have a check on the people in case the people voted for someone whom the leaders do not like.

WE DO NOT VOTE DIRECTLY FOR THE PRESIDENT UNDER THE ELECTORAL COLLEGE

Choose the right word for each blank.

amendment   changed   college

SOLUTION:

Any part of the Constitution may be _____ by

_____. If enough voters want to do away with the electoral

_____, they can tell their senators and representatives.
The senators and representatives can then propose an amendment.

CASE 15

Citizens are Supreme

PROBLEM:

The leaders of the new country do not want the army to run the government.

BACKGROUND:

The people know many military governments in Europe which take away citizens' freedoms.

THE MILITARY LEADERS MUST OBEY THE PRESIDENT

Choose the right word for each blank.

| Commander-in-Chief | higher | President |

SOLUTION:

The Constitution says that the _____ is

_____ - _____ - _____ of all of the **armed**

forces. This makes him or her _____ in rank than any general
or admiral.

CASE 16

Treaties — The President and the Senate Share Power

PROBLEM:

Many writers of the Constitution do not want the President to be able to **sign a**
treaty with a foreign country without the approval of Congress.

BACKGROUND:

The leaders of the country want many of the President's actions **approved by**
another branch of government.

THE SENATE MUST APPROVE OF THE PRESIDENT'S TREATY

Choose the right word for each blank.

| treaty | Senate | approved |

SOLUTION:

The Constitution says that any _____ signed by the **President**

must be _____ by ⅔ of the _____.

CHAPTER 13

What Did You Learn?

ONE: VOCABULARY

Read each sentence. Write the word which best completes the meaning of the sentence.

1. Presidents are _____ at their party's conventions.   [nominated, numbered]

2. Presidents who break laws may be

   _____.   [infected, impeached]

3. The number of votes that the people cast

   is called the _____ vote.   [pretty, popular]

4. The _____ college selects the President.   [electoral, energy]

5. _____ means being found guilty of something illegal.   [Conviction, Catching]

6. The _____ are members of the electoral college.   [eagles, electors]

7. The Democrats and the Republicans are our two

   main political _____.   [parties, pictures]

8. The electoral _____ is the vote by state for the President.   [vote, vine]

9. Ted Field is the Democratic Party's

   _____ for Mayor.   [cowboy, candidate]

TWO: UNDERSTANDING THE FACTS

1. Fill in the right word.

1. There is an election for President every _____ years.

    A. 2   C. 4

    B. 6   D. 3

2. Each political party picks a _____ to run for President.

    A. senator   C. lawyer

    B. candidate   D. judge

3. The _____ _____ selects the President after the people vote.

    A. electoral college   C. minister

    B. cabinet   D. senate

4. The total people's vote for President is called

the _____.

    A. nomination   C. popular vote

    B. convention   D. selection

5. The first step in firing a President who does something against the law

is _____.

    A. impeachment   C. awards

    B. jury selecting   D. appeals

2. True or False?

Circle T or F:

1. States with many people have more electoral
votes than states with fewer people.   T F
2. The President and the Vice President are
the only officials who are elected
by electoral vote.   T F

3. If Presidents are impeached, they must
quit right away.   T   F
4. Both Houses of Congress take part in removing
a President who does illegal things.   T   F
5. We had a President who was impeached, but
he did not lose his job.   T   F

3. Put these steps in the right order.

_____ A. The members of the House of Representatives think that the President commits a bad crime.

_____ B. The President loses his or her job.

_____ C. The House of Representatives votes to impeach the President.

_____ D. The Senate votes that the President is guilty of the crime.

THREE: LEARNING THE LANGUAGE

1. Base words. We use base words with different endings to make new words. (Both verbs and nouns).

Base Word	Action Word (verb)	Subject (noun)
1. elect	electoral	elec*tion*
2. convict	convicted	convic*tion*
3. nominate	nominated	nomina*tion*
4. Impeach	impeached	impeach*ment*

Use one of the word forms in each sentence.

1. The e_____ was held to choose the President.

2. Anita Campo was n_____ for mayor by the Republicans.

3. I _____ is to accuse a President of bad conduct.

4. President Andrew Johnson was not c_____ of illegal acts.

14

Article III
The Judicial Branch

KEY WORDS

constitutional — A law which the Constitution says is proper. This is decided by
  judges.
  The court declared the law *constitutional*.

unconstitutional — A law which goes against the meaning of the Constitution. This
  is decided by judges.
  If the Supreme Court says that a law is *unconstitutional,* the law does not apply.
  The court decided that the unfair law was *unconstitutional*.

appeal — To take a case to a higher court for "another chance."
  The man *appealed* the court's decision.

District Court — The lowest court in the federal court system.
  Most of the federal cases are tried here.
  The *district court* heard the case.

Court of Appeals — A court that hears cases which are appealed from the district
  courts.
  Ms. Jones was so upset by the decision of the District Court that she went to the
  Court of Appeals.

Supreme Court — The highest court in our country.
The Supreme Court has the final decision as to whether a law is constitutional. After Ms. Jones lost her case in the Court of Appeals, she went to the *Supreme Court*.

checks and balances — The ability of each of the three branches of government to stop each other from getting too much power.
The President showed an example of *checks and balances* when he did not sign a bill that Congress wanted to become a law.

judicial review — This is what happens when judges decide whether a law is constitutional. They must decide on what they believe the writers of the Constitution meant in each case.
Judicial review is the way our Constitution changes the most.

The third partner in our federal government is the JUDICIAL BRANCH. Article III tells us all about this branch.

The Constitution says that the federal court system is the Supreme Court and any lower courts set up by Congress.

The federal court system hears cases which involve *federal* laws. So, when people break federal laws, their cases go to federal courts.

There are separate court systems for cities and states. For example, if a person breaks a state law, they would be tried in a state court.

How the Federal Courts are set up
These are the three levels of federal courts:

District Court
Court of Appeals
Supreme Court

District Courts
There are more *District Courts* than any other federal court. They are the first step in the federal court system. Most of the federal cases start here. District courts are in our largest cities.

Sometimes if people lose their cases in a District Court they can take their cases to a higher court. This is called an *appeal*.

The Court of Appeals is the next higher court. But people who appeal the case must find a mistake that the District Court judge made in their trial.

Court of Appeals

The *Court of Appeals* hears cases that have been appealed from the District Courts. If the person on trial loses again in the Court of Appeals, the person can try to convince the Supreme Court to take the case. The judges in the Court of Appeals must make a mistake before someone can appeal a case.

Supreme Court

The *Supreme Court* can choose its cases. It hears cases that it thinks are very important. This is because the Supreme Court has the power to decide whether a law is constitutional.

There are only nine judges on the Supreme Court so their time must be carefully spent. These nine judges vote carefully on each case that is heard.

The Supreme Court is the court where some special cases must begin. These are suits between states or cases that deal with other countries.

How federal judges get their jobs

The President picks federal judges. The President must pick somebody who is good enough to be a federal judge. The *Senate* must approve of federal judges before they get the job.

If the President chooses a friend who is not fit for the job, the Senate refuses to okay the choice. This is one of our government's checks and balances that we will study in Chapter 16.

Federal judges may hold their jobs for life if they desire. But they may be removed from office by impeachment and conviction if they are found guilty of bad behavior.

Duties of the Federal Courts

The main job of the federal courts is to decide cases on federal laws that might have been broken.

Judicial Review

Judicial review is an important duty of the federal court system. Judicial review means that the court is the final "umpire" to decide whether a law is constitutional.

The meaning of the Constitution changes most under the power of *judicial review*. This is because of the large numbers of cases that arise. Every time a judge decides a case, the judge looks at how previous cases that were similar have been decided.

So each time a case is decided, it becomes a guide for similar cases.

<u>Checks and balances</u>

Judicial review is another of our system's checks and balances. If Congress passes a law that is unconstitutional, then the court system can do away with the law.

The Supreme Court does not decide whether laws are constitutional when they are passed by Congress. A case must be started in the court system before the court rules whether a law is constitutional.

CASE 17

Another Chance in Court

PROBLEM:

A person who is on trial in a federal court might not get a fair trial because of a judge's mistake or prejudice.

BACKGROUND:

When the leaders write the Constitution, many larger countries have unfair courts. Their judges are friends of the king or owe their jobs to him.

The writers of our Constitution want the courts to be fair to everybody. We have the right to another trial if the judge makes a mistake.

ANOTHER CHANCE IN COURT

Choose the right word for each blank.

reasons   court   appeal

SOLUTION:

The Constitution lets someone _____ to a higher

_____ if he or she has good _____ for the appeal.

CASE 18

Who Can Become a Federal Judge?

PROBLEM:

The Constitution does not list any requirements of age, education, or experience for someone to become a federal judge. What is to stop the President from selecting a friend or neighbor who is not good enough for this important job?

BACKGROUND:

When the Constitution is written, there are few law schools. People who want to be lawyers study law by working in a law office.

THE SENATE "OK's" THE PRESIDENT'S CHOICES FOR JUDGE

Choose the right words for each blank.

President   good   Constitution

SOLUTION:

The _____ says that the Senate must approve of anyone whom

the _____ nominates to the federal court system. This

makes sure that they are really _____ enough for the job.

> **FREE MINIFACT**
> Since the Supreme Court is like an "umpire," a good way to remember that there are nine justices on the Supreme Court is to remember that there are nine people on a baseball team.

CHAPTER 14

What Did You Learn?

ONE: VOCABULARY

1. Write a sentence using each key word. If you need help, read the definitions at the beginning of Chapter 14.

constitutional	Court of Appeals
unconstitutional	Supreme Court
appeal	checks and balances
District Court	judicial review

1. _____

2. _____

3. _____

4. _____

5. _____

6. _____

7. _____

8. _____

2. Can you unscramble these words?

1. NPSIDREET _____ This is who selects (nominates) the federal judges.

2. LANOITUTITSNOC _____ What a federal law must be.

3. LAAPEP _____ You can do this sometimes if you lose a case in court.

4. TROUC _____ Cases are heard here.

HINTS

constitutional	court
appeal	President

112

TWO: UNDERSTANDING THE FACTS

1. Fill in the right letter.

1. The three levels of federal courts are _____.

    A. National, American, and Trial
    B. District, Court of Appeals, Supreme Court
    C. Executive, Legislative, and Judicial

2. Somebody would appeal his court case if _____.

    A. he loses his case in a lower court and he shows that the judge has made a mistake.
    B. he wins his case.
    C. he does not like the courtroom.

3. The _____ may decide whether it wants to take a case on appeal.

    A. District Court
    B. Court of Appeals
    C. Supreme Court

4. Judicial review is when the judge _____.

    A. sentences a person to a long time in jail.
    B. decides whether a case is constitutional and that decision is used in similar future cases.
    C. refuses to let a person testify in court.

5. The _____ hears the most cases because it is where federal cases begin.

    A. District Court
    B. Court of Appeals
    C. Supreme Court

2. True or False?

Circle T or F:

1. There are three levels of federal courts.   T F
2. The President picks judges for the federal courts. T F
3. Federal judges hold their jobs for four years.   T F
4. The Senate has to approve of judges
   who are picked for the federal courts.   T F
5. The Supreme Court rules if a law is unconstitutional
   when it is passed by Congress.   T F

3. Writing Project:

Describe the three levels of Courts:

        District Court   Court of Appeals
        Supreme Court

_____

_____

_____

_____

_____

_____

_____

THREE: LEARNING THE LANGUAGE

When did it happen?

Past tense = yesterday.   Present tense = today or every day.   Future tense = tomorrow.

Example: I got up at 7:00 yesterday. past

              I get up at 7:00 present

              I will get up at 7:00 future

Write "past, present," or future" in each space.

1. I brushed my teeth. _____

2. I comb my hair. _____

3. I ate breakfast. _____

4. I will get up at 6:00 tomorrow. _____

5. I brush my teeth. _____

HOW A BILL BECOMES A LAW

15

How A Bill Becomes A Law

KEY WORDS

committee — A group of people picked to do a definite job.
We are on the mayor's "Clean the City *Committee*."

veto — To vote against.
Presidents *veto* bills that they do not want to become laws.

majority — More than one half of something.
The *majority* of the committee wanted John as its leader.

bill — A proposal that Congress would like to become a law.
The *bill* started in the Senate.

quorum — More than one half of the total membership.
There must be a *quorum* before the House can vote on a bill.

A Bill's Path to Become a Law
A bill must go through many steps before it becomes a law. If the bill fails in any of these steps, it dies and does not become a law.

Where does a bill start?

Both houses of Congress must agree to a bill before it can become a law. They vote for or against the bill. The bill may start in either the House of Representatives or the Senate unless it is a bill about money. A money bill must begin in the House of Representatives.

Voting on the bill

Before a bill may be voted upon, there must be a *quorum* present in each House.

Here is the path of a typical bill:

1. A representative wants to pass a bill to build a new road for the people in the home district.
2. The representative drops the bill into a mailbox called a hopper.
   (See Figure 1.)
3. When the bills in the hopper are examined, they are sent to the proper committee; in this case — the *Public Works Committee.*
   (See Figure 2.)
4. The representatives on the committee vote on whether the bill should be brought for a vote by the entire House of Representatives.
5. The bill is brought to the whole House of Representatives for a vote.
   (See Figure 3.)
6. If a simple majority (one more than one-half of the representatives) vote for the bill, it has "passed the House of Representatives."
7. The bill now goes to the Public Works Committee of the Senate for them to decide on it.
8. If the Senate Public Works Committee approves, the bill is brought to the whole Senate for a vote.
   (See Figure 4.)
9. If a majority of the members of the Senate vote for the bill, it is sent to the President for signature.
10. The President signs the bill if the President wants it to become a law.
    (See Figure 5.)
    The President vetoes it if he or she does not like it.
11. If the President vetoes the bill, it may still become a law if ⅔ of *both* houses of Congress vote for it again.
    Steps 1-10 must be completed for the bill to become a law. If the bill fails at any of these steps, it "dies" and does not become a law. Step 11 gives the bill another chance.

As we learned, the federal court system has the last word. Let us say that someone sues under the law. If the case goes to the Supreme Court, and they rule the law unconstitutional, the law is dead.

CASE 19

A Bill Must Be Strong to Stay Alive

PROBLEM:
Too many bills can "die" because there are so many steps before a bill becomes a law.

BACKGROUND:
Many of the countries had bad or unfair laws when the Constitution was written. These laws were easy to pass. They were also cruelly enforced.

A BILL MUST BE STRONG TO STAY ALIVE

Choose the right words for each blank.

        Constitution   law   needed

SOLUTIONS:

The _____ makes sure that a bill is **really**

_____ and fair before it passes to become a _____.

CHAPTER 15

What Did You Learn?

ONE: VOCABULARY

1. Complete each sentence with a key word that fits the definition.

1. A _____ is a proposal that Congress would like to become a law.　　[treaty, bill]

2. _____ means more than one-half.　　[Majority, Minority]

3. A _____ is a group of people picked to do a definite job.　　[committee, school]

4. _____ means to cancel with a single vote.　　[veto, video]

2. Match these words.

Fill in the right letter.

1. veto _____
2. majority _____
3. House of Representatives _____
4. Revenue _____
5. Law _____

A. A bill that has to do with money (revenue) begins here.

B. One more than half of a group.

C. What a bill becomes if it passes.

D. A President does this to a bill that he does not like.

E. Money collected by the government.

TWO: UNDERSTANDING THE FACTS

1. Fill in the right words.

1. _____ is money collected by the government.

　　A. Committee　　C. Revenue
　　B. Judicial　　D. Senator

2. A bill may start in either house of Congress unless the bill is about

_____.

        A. farming   C. labor

        B. revenue   D. defense

3. _____ members in each house must vote for a bill to pass it.

        A. A dozen   C. A majority of

        B. Thirty   D. One hundred

4. If a President does not like a bill passed by Congress, he

or she _____ it.

        A. frames   C. files

        B. vetoes   D. signs

5. If the President likes the bill, he or she _____ it.

        A. frames   C. files

        B. vetoes   D. signs

2. True or False?

Circle T or F:

1. The President may pass a bill by himself.   T F
2. A bill goes through many steps before it becomes a law.   T F
3. Ten members of either house make a majority.   T F
4. A bill must pass both houses before it can go to the President for signing.   T F
5. The Supreme Court rules on each law as it is passed to see if it is constitutional.   T F

3. Put these steps in the right order.

_____ A. The President signs the bill and it becomes a law.

_____ B. A majority of the Senate and House of Representatives vote for the bill.

_____ C. A bill to help farmers is started in the Senate.

THREE: LEARNING THE LANGUAGE

Change each statement into a question.

Example: STATEMENT — A majority is more than one-half of something.

QUESTION — Is a majority more than one-half of something?

1. STATEMENT — The President vetoes a bill he does not like.

   QUESTION — _____

2. STATEMENT — A bill must pass both Houses of Congress.

   QUESTION — _____

3. STATEMENT — The Supreme Court can rule that laws are unconstitutional.

   QUESTION — _____

4. STATEMENT — Senator Smith is on the Labor Committee.

   QUESTION — _____

16

Our System of Checks and Balances

KEY WORDS

branches (of our government) — The three parts of our national government.
The three *branches* of the United States government are LEGISLATIVE, EXECUTIVE, and JUDICIAL.

power — The ability or right to do certain things.
The President has the *power* to sign bills into laws.

appointment — A President's choices for jobs; nominations.
Most senators like the President's new *appointment* for federal justice.

The leaders of the new country were afraid to give the President too much power. This was because of their hard times with King George III.

This is why the writers of the new Constitution made three separate branches in the new government.

Three branches of government
These are the three branches of our federal government:
> Legislative
> Executive
> Judicial

Each branch can stop or control what the other branches do. (The power of each branch is *checked* or *balanced* against the powers of the others.)

Checks against the executive (President)

How Congress can check the President:
The President cannot sign a treaty with another country unless ⅔ of the Senate votes for it.

Presidents do not make the laws. They sign bills that are passed by Congress.

Congress can pass a law without the President's signature with a ⅔ majority vote.

The Senate must approve of many of the President's appointments (federal justices, cabinet members, etc.).

Congress may fire a President if that person is guilty of high crimes (IMPEACHMENT PROCESS).

Finally, Congress has the power to vote money to carry out the President's policies. They can also refuse to give the President money.

How the courts can check the President:
The courts can declare laws that the President has signed *unconstitutional*.

Although the President picks the federal justices, the President cannot fire them. This means that federal justices do not have to obey the President.

Checks against Congress:
The President can refuse to sign bills that Congress has passed.

The Supreme Court can rule laws that Congress has passed *unconstitutional*.

Checks against the court system:
The President must appoint the members of the federal court system.

The Senate must approve of the President's choice.

A federal justice may be impeached and convicted by Congress if the justice breaks the law.

CASE 20

Checks and Balances on the President

PROBLEM:

The President does not have as much power as rulers of some other countries have.

BACKGROUND:

The people do not want the President to have too much power because of their bad experience with King George III.

OUR COUNTRY'S POWER IS DIVIDED INTO THREE PARTS

Choose the right word for each blank.

power   stops   branches

SOLUTION:

Each branch of government has ways to stop unwise actions of the other

_____ (CHECKS AND BALANCES).

This _____ any branch from getting too much _____.

124

CHAPTER 16

What Did You Learn?

ONE: VOCABULARY

1. Use the key words to complete the paragraph.

           branches   appointment   power

There are three _____ of government. The President has the

_____ to make _____s.

2. Can you unscramble these words?

   1. REOPW _____   The ability or right to do
                                         certain things.

   2. TNOPAPIMETNS _____
                                         A President's choices for jobs.

   3. KHECCS _____   The ability of one branch of
                                         government to stop another
                                         branch from doing something.

HINTS

   appointments   power
   checks

TWO: UNDERSTANDING THE FACTS

1. Fill in the right words.

   1. The leaders of our country were afraid to give the President too much

        _____ because of their hard times with King George.

           A. power   C. money
           B. respect   D. to eat

2. Each branch of government has ways to _____ the power of the other two branches.

        A. increase   C. check

        B. charge   D. steal

3. The President cannot sign a treaty with another country unless ⅔ of the

_____ agrees to it.

        A. Senate   C. Supreme Court

        B. Vice President   D. governor

4. _____ can declare laws that the President has signed "unconstitutional."

        A. Congress   C. The states

        B. Citizens   D. The Supreme Court

5. Although the President picks federal judges, the President cannot

_____ them.

        A. hire   C. fire

        B. talk to   D. see

2. True or False?

Circle T or F:

1. The writers of the Constitution wanted to divide the country's powers into three parts.	T	F
2. There are no checks on the President's powers.	T	F
3. There is a way for Congress to pass a bill even if the President vetoes it.	T	F
4. The Senate must agree to many of the President's appointments.	T	F
5. There is no way to fire a federal judge who does illegal things.	T	F

3. Checks and balances. Tell which branch has these checks and balances:

use these letters: L = Legislative
                       E = Executive
                       J = Judicial

Example: ___E___ The President is the head of this branch.

1. _____ Declares laws unconstitutional.

2. _____ Vetoes unwanted bills.

3. _____ Must approve some of the President's appointments.

4. _____ Hired by the President, but cannot be fired by the President.

5. _____ Can impeach and convict a President or federal judge who does illegal things.

THREE: LEARNING THE LANGUAGE

Rhyming Words.

1. Use the "an" ending to complete each word. The first one is done for you.

   r a n   c____   f____   m____   t____

2. Read the sentences below. Use the words above to complete the sentences.

   a. The dog _____ away.

   b. George Washington was a great _____.

   c. Open the soup _____.

   d. The _____ makes us cool.

   e. Andrea painted her room _____.

17

Articles IV-VII
(The Remaining Articles)

KEY WORDS

amend — To change or add to something.
The people wanted to *amend* the Constitution.

amendment — Something added to a document. A change in the document.
The Senate voted on the *amendment* to the bill.

proposal — What someone would like to do.
The first step in making an amendment is a *proposal*.

ratify — To make a proposal official.
The final step in making an amendment to the Constitution is to *ratify* the amendment.

legislative — The part of the government that makes the laws.
Senators are members of the *legislative* branch of government.

Article IV

What Article IV is about:

Article IV tells us how the federal government and the state governments share power. It also tells how the states must treat each other's laws.

Here are some of the main points in this article:

The official acts of each state shall be accepted in the other states.

Here are two examples:
   a. If a driver lives in New York and drives in New Jersey, his New York driver's license and license plates will be legal.
   b. If a couple lives in a state in which it is legal to get married at seventeen, their marriage license will be good if they move to a state where the age to get married is the same or higher.

If a person commits a serious crime in one state and escapes to another state, that person is returned to the state in which the crime was committed.

Congress has the power to admit new states.

Congress has the power to make rules for the land that the United States owns.

The United States promises each state an elected government.

Article V

What Article V is about:

This article tells how to AMEND (change) the Constitution.

There are two steps to an amendment:

It must be PROPOSED (suggested).

It is then RATIFIED (approved).

Two ways an amendment may be proposed:
By a ⅔ vote in each House.
        OR
By ⅔ of all of the states asking for it.

Two ways an amendment may be ratified:
By ¾ of the state legislatures.
        OR
By special meetings in ¾ of the states.

Article VI

What Article VI is about:
The money that the country owed before the Constitution was adopted will be repaid.

The Constitution is the highest law in the country.

A state may not have a law that does not agree with the federal Constitution. For example, the Constitution says that the governor of a state may pick somebody to replace a senator who dies or quits. A state may not pass a law that calls for a special election to pick a new senator.

Any person who works for the federal government must promise to obey our Constitution.

People of any religion may hold jobs in the government.

Article VII

This is an unusual article because it only tells how the Constitution is to be passed.

Since the Constitution already has been passed, this article is not used to create new laws. It says that:

Nine or more states must ratify (approve) the Constituion before it exists.

It then says that all of the states *did* agree to it.

CASE 21

Only U.S. Money Allowed!

PROBLEM:

A state wants to pass a law that will let the state make its oown money.

BACKGROUND:

The Constitution says that only the federal government may coin and print money. The Constitution also says that a state law must agree with the federal Constitution.

STATES MAY NOT PRINT THEIR OWN MONEY

Choose the right word for each blank.

       state   money   Constitution

SOLUTION:

The state cannot print its own _____ because the

_____ law must not go against the federal _____.

CHAPTER 17

What Did You Learn?

ONE: VOCABULARY

amend   ratify

amendment   legislative

proposal

1. Use the right letter to complete the key words in these sentences:

1. The people want to _____mend the Constitution.   [a, e]

2. _____atify means to make a proposal official.   [R, S]

3. Congress is the _____legislative branch of government.   [r, l]

4. The _____mendment was added to the Constitution.   [e, a]

5. The first step in making an amendment is
    a _____roposal.   [p, t]

2. Crossword. Fill in the blanks from the following words. Use the definitions to help you.

acts   crime

government   states

DEFINITIONS

Across

1. A state must have an elected

    _____ .

2. States accept other states;

    _____ .

Down

3. A person who commits a _____ in New York and escapes to New Jersey may be returned to New York for trial.

4. Congress can admit new _____ to the United States.

TWO: UNDERSTANDING THE FACTS

1. Fill in the right words.

1. Congress has the power to admit new _____ to the United States.

    A. cars   C. states
    B. ambassadors   D. judges

2. The United States promises each state an

_____ government.
    A. elected   C. old
    B. empty   D. alien

3. The two steps to make an amendment to the Constitution are

_____ and ratification.
    A. publication   C. proposal
    B. display   D. veto

4. The Constitution is the highest _____ in the country.
    A. law   C. hill
    B. church   D. book

5. A person who works for the federal government must

_____ the Constitution.
    A. memorize   C. copy
    B. obey   D. record

2. True or False?

Circle T or F:

1. There are twenty articles in the Constitution.   T   F
2. The federal government and the state
   governments share some powers.   T   F
3. Someone who robs a bank in California and runs
   to Nevada cannot be punished for the crime.   T   F
4. Congress can say nothing about what kinds
   of governments states may have.   T   F
5. State laws must agree with the United States
   Constitution.   T   F

THREE: LEARNING THE LANGUAGE

Word endings. We use base words with different endings to make new words.

Base Word	New Word
amend	amendment
propose	proposal
ratify	ratification
legislate	legislative
approve	approval

Use one of the word forms in each sentence.

1. Many people want an a_____t to give women equal rights.

2. Congress is the l_____e branch of government.

3. The President signs the bill to show his a_____l.

4. The first step in getting a new Amendment is to p_____e it.

5. The final step in getting a new amendment is r_____n.

18

Amendments To The Constitution

KEY WORDS

petition — To ask the government for something.
A petition may be signed by many people or just one person.
He signed the *petition* for a new park.

interpret — To tell the meaning of.
The Supreme Court *interprets* the meaning of the Constitution.

warrant — A legal paper signed by a judge.
The most common *warrant* gives the police permission to search a person or his house. The policeman had a *warrant* to search that house.

grand jury — A special jury that sees if there is enough evidence to accuse someone of a crime.
The *grand jury* said that there was not enough evidence to bring Tom to trial for robbery.

bail — Money that is put up by a person accused of a crime.
People accused of a crime put up *bail* so they can stay out of jail until their trial.
John put up $1000 *bail* so he would not have to stay in jail until the date of his trial.

prohibited — Not allowed or not legal.
  Smoking is *prohibited* in many public places.

term — The number of years that a person serves in a public job.
  The President has four years in each *term*.

The Bill of Rights

The Bill of Rights is almost a part of the original Constitution. The Bill of Rights make up the first ten amendments to the Constitution. They make sure that we have many of our rights and freedoms.

Here are some of the rights that the first ten amendments give us:

Amendment I:
Freedom of religion.
  Freedom of the press (books, newspapers, magazines, television, etc.).
  Freedom to meet in public or private.
  Freedom to ask the government to change something if we feel that it is wrong. (RIGHT OF PETITION).

Amendment II:
Tells about the right of the people to have a state military (militia). Some people say that this means that each citizen can have guns. But not everybody agrees on this.

Amendment III:
This says that we are not forced to have soldiers stay in our houses.
  Of course, if the soldier is your brother, he can stay in your house. (*IF* he has permission to be away from the army base!)

Amendment IV:
The police may not search our houses unless they have a *warrant*. A warrant is a legal paper signed by a judge which gives the police permission to search a house or car.
  The warrant must give a definite reason for the search. It must also list the exact place that is searched.

Amendment V:
This is a very important amendment. People who are on trial use it very often.
  These are its main ideas:
        The courts cannot try a person unless a grand jury finds enough evidence.

If the court says that someone is not guilty of a crime, the government cannot bring them to court again for the same crime. Of course, if they commit a similar crime in the future, the will be tried for the new crime.

If the country, state, or city needs a person's land, they may purchase it at a fair price.

People who are on trial do not have to give evidence against themselves. (It is up to the government to prove that they have done wrong. People are innocent until they are proved guilty.)

Amendment VI:

Amendment VI tells us that:

A person should have a speedy and a fair trial.

People must be able to hear the exact charges against them.

People have a right to be present when anyone speaks against them at their trial.

People also have a right to bring their own witnesses and their own lawyer to help them at their trial.

Amendment VII:

This amendment gives us the right to a trial by jury. A *jury* usually has twelve ordinary people who find out the facts in a case.

Amendment VIII:

Amendment VIII gives us these rights:

There can be no cruel or unusual punishment for people convicted of crimes.

The courts must not ask for too much bail.

The fines must fit the crime.

Amendment IX:

This amendment says that we have many rights that the Constitution does not list.

For example, we have the right to breathe. It is not in the Constitution because it would be impossible to list all of the rights.

Amendment X:

There are some powers that the Constitution does not give to the federal government.

These powers belong to the people and the states. This is true unless it is a power that the Constitution prohibits.

Amendments Passed After the Bill of Rights

Amendment XI:
This amendment says that the federal courts cannot try these kinds of cases:
When a citizen of one state sues another state.
When a foreigner sues one of our states.

Amendment XII:
This amendment sets up the rules for the electoral college in the election of a President.

Amendment XIII:
This amendment stopped slavery.

Amendment XIV:
Amendment XIV says that:
All people who are born in this country are citizens.
A state cannot make any law which takes away a citizen's rights.
The number of people in each state is used to figure out how many members there are in the House of Representatives.

Amendment XV:
Any citizen can vote if that person meets the voting requirement. This is true no matter what the person's race or color might be.

Amendment XVI:
This gives Congress the right to collect an income tax.

Amendment XVII:
The people of each state can vote directly for their United States senators.

Amendment XVIII:
This amendment prohibited liquor in the United States. It was cancelled by the Twenty-first Amendment.

Amendment XIX:
Women can vote in all elections.

Amendment XX:
A President's term starts on January 20 at noon.

Amendment XXI

The Eighteenth Amendment which prohibited liquor was repealed (cancelled) by this amendment.

Amendment XXII

A President may only have two terms in office but can serve in office for ten (10) years if he or she finishes the term of a previous President.

Amendment XXIII

The people who live in Washington, D.C. may vote for the President and Vice President. They could not do this before this Amendment.

Amendment XXIV

States may not make voters pay a tax before they can vote.

Amendment XXV

If there is no Vice President because he or she died or quit, the President chooses the new Vice President.

This choice must be approved by both Houses of Congress

Amendment XXVI

People who are eighteen (18) years of age may vote. Before that, you had to be twenty-one (21) in most states.

Amendment XVII

The pay to the members of the House and Senate cannot change until after an election of Representatives has occurred.

As you can see there are twenty-seven amendments to the Constitution. This is not many if you realize that the Constitution is over 200 years old, and the way people live changed so much through the years.

The Constitution is really changing every day. Every time there is a Court decision, the meaning of the Constitution changes. The judge must decide what the writers of the Constitution meant.

These decisions are put in books for judges to use in deciding cases. So our Constitution is almost like a living thing since it is so flexible. But, for all of its flexibility, it forms a rock-solid base for our democratic ideals.

SOMETHING TO THINK ABOUT

Your children and your children's children will live quite differently than we do. The Constitution will still be able to help them govern because of its amazing ability to adapt to new inventions and new ideas.

CHAPTER 18

What Did You Learn?

ONE: VOCABULARY

Circle the correct meaning.

Example:

Term	(time in office)	clock	calendar

1. **petition**	fly	jump	ask
2. **interpret**	tell	color	paint
3. **warrant**	legal paper	art paper	newspaper
4. **grand jury**	judge	special jury	victim
5. **bail**	bucket	baseball	money
6. **prohibited**	not allowed	lost	sold

TWO: UNDERSTANDING THE FACTS

1. Fill in the right word.

1. The Constitution does not say that we have freedom of _____.

   A. speech   C. press
   B. crime   D. religion

2. We have the freedom to ask the government to _____ something that we think is wrong.

   A. keep   C. add
   B. print   D. change

3. A _____ is a legal paper signed by a judge which gives permission for the police to search a house.

   A. warrant   C. magazine
   B. book   D. jury

4. A person must have a fair and _____ trial.

      A. speedy   C. televised

      B. private   D. slow

5. We have _____ rights that are not listed in the Constitution.

      A. no   C. 65

      B. many   D. 12

2. True or False?

Circle T or F:

1. The United States has an official religion.   T   F
2. People who win their court cases cannot be tried again for the same crime.   T   F
3. A person on trial must give complete evidence against himself.   T   F
4. Congress may not collect an income tax.   T   F
5. We have one amendment that cancelled another amendment.   T   F
6. A President may have five terms in office.   T   F
7. Judges interpret the Constitution.   T   F
8. States can charge people a poll tax before they can vote.   T   F
9. People must be 21 years old before they can vote for President.   T   F
10. The Constitution is really changing every time a judge interprets it.   T   F

THREE: LEARNING THE LANGUAGE

Antonyms. An antonym is a word that means the opposite of another word.

Example: hot   cold

Circle the antonym for each word.

Example: good   kind   (bad)   tall

1. many   honey   money   few

2. lose   find   cry   skip

3. innocent   fat   guilty   smart

4. speedy   fast   hard   slow

5. cruel   short   pretty   nice

6. pass   fail   teacher   ship

7. stop   go   jump   run

8. hire   raise   fire   load

19

Our Flag

KEY WORDS

symbol — A thing used to stand for something else.
The flag is a *symbol* of our country.

display — To show.
We *display* the flag at our meetings.

vertical — Upright. Up and down.
The flag pole is *vertical*.

Our flag is a symbol of glory. It stands for our country's ideals. It is an important part of our country's history.

The red in the flag stands for courage; the white for liberty; and the blue for loyalty.

The thirteen stripes stand for the original thirteen states.

A new star is added to the flag every time a state is added to the United States. That is why the flag has 50 stars — one for each state. Many people still remember the 48-star flag. That was our flag before Alaska and Hawaii were admitted as states.

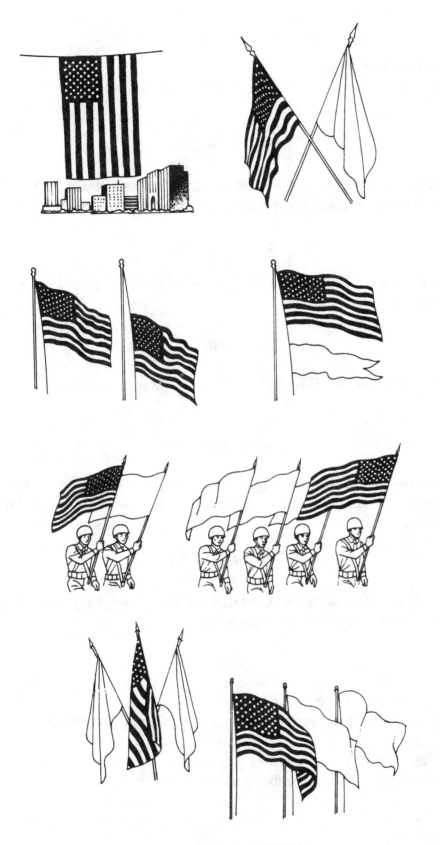

HOW TO DISPLAY THE FLAG

145

How to display the Flag:

When the flag flies over the middle of a street, it should hang vertically (up and down).

(See Figure 1.)

When the American flag is displayed with another flag, the staffs (poles) should cross. The American flag's staff should be in front of the other flag's staff.

(See Figure 2.)

The President may order flags to fly at HALF STAFF. This happens when a very important person dies.

(See Figure 3.)

When the American flag flies with state flags, the American flag must be higher.

(See Figure 4.)

Sometimes the American flag is displayed in a parade with other state or city flags. Then the American flag should either be on the right of the other flag or in front of it.

(See Figure 5.)

When flags of two or more countries are displayed, they should be the same height. They should also be the same size.

(See Figure 6.)

The flag should fly every day.
It is especially important for the flag to fly on holidays.
The flag should not be used for advertising.
The flag should not touch the ground.
Worn out flags should be burned.

CHAPTER 19

What Did You Learn?

ONE: VOCABULARY

1. Use the key words to complete the paragraph.

       symbol   vertical   display

The flag is a _____ of our country. There are rules that

tell us how to _____ the flag. Most flag poles are

_____.

2. Can you unscramble these words?

   1. PRSTIES _____ There are thirteen of
                                    these on our flag.

   2. SRAT _____ The flag has one for each state.

   3. YPLDSAI _____ To show.

   4. DAVERSINGTI _____ A flag may not be used for this.

   5. DNUREB _____ A worn-out flag should

      be _____.

                    HINTS
           stars   display
           stripes   advertising
           burned

147

TWO: UNDERSTANDING THE FACTS

1. Fill in the right word.

   1. Our flag has one _____ for each state in our country.

        A. stripe   C. star
        B. color   D. type

   2. The flag is a _____ of our country.

        A. symbol   C. picture
        B. copy   D. cartoon

   3. The flag has _____ stars.

        A. 100   C. 13
        B. 26   D. 50

2. True or False?

Circle T or F:

1. The flag has an important part in our history.   T F
2. There are rules about displaying the flag.   T F
3. The President may order flags to fly at half staff when an important person dies.   T F
4. The United States flag may never be displayed with flags of other countries.   T F

THREE: LEARNING THE LANGUAGE

Rhyming Words.

1. Use the "ay" ending to complete each word. The first one is done for you.

      p l a y   s_____   p_____   h_____   d_____

2. Read the sentences below. Use the words above to complete the sentences.

    a. Children like to _____ baseball.

    b. Horses eat _____.

    c. The flag should fly during the _____.

    d. Did you _____ for your meal?

    e. We _____ hello to our friends.

Glossary

adjourn—To call an end to a meeting. It was late so they wanted to *adjourn* the meeting.

alien—A person who lives in a country, but is not a citizen. Jose is an *alien* because he was born in Mexico. He did not become a citizen.

ambassador—A person who speaks for a country in another country. Mr. Jones is our *ambassador* to Mexico.

amend—To change or add to something. We want to *amend* the Constitution.

amendment—Something that is added to the Ctnstitution. Many people want a new *amendment* to assure women equal rights.

appeal—To take a case to a higher court for "another chance." Mr. Harris *appealed* his case to a higher court.

appointment—A choice for jobs; nominations. The President's new *appointment* for federal judge was announced.

approve—To show that you are satisfied with something. The President *approved* the bill by signing it.

Articles of Confederation—Our first constitution. The *Articles of Confederation* did not work well.

assemble—When a group of people meet in one place. Our team will *assemble* in the park.

attorney—A lawyer; a person trained in law who can represent us in court. Henry hired an *attorney* to go with him to court.

attorney general—The cabinet member who is the head of the Justice Department. The *attorney general* is the chief lawyer for the United States.

bail—Money that is put up by a person accused of a crime. Tom posted *bail* so that he could stay out of jail until his trial.

bill—An idea that Congress would like to become a law. Senator Chavez wants to start a *bill* to help the farmers.

branches (of our government)—The three parts of our government. The Legislative, Executive, and Judicial *branches* of our government work well.

cabinet member—A person who is in charge of one of the departments in the Executive branch. The attorney general is a *cabinet member*.

candidate—A person who runs for office. Both parties select a *candidate* for President.

capital—The city that is the center of government. Washington, D.C. is our *capital*.

Capitol—The dome-shaped building in which Congress meets. The Senate and House of Representatives meet in the *Capitol* Building.

checks and balances—How each of the three branches of government can stop each other from getting too much power. The President's veto is an example of *checks and balances*.

citizen—Someone who is a member of a country. Tom is a *citizen* because he was born in this country.

colonist—A person who lives in a country that is run by another country. George Washington was an English *colonist* before the Revolutionary War.

colony—A country that is run by another country. Our land used to be a *colony* of England.

Commander-in-Chief—The person at the highest level of leadership. The President is *Commander-in-Chief* of the armed forces.

commerce—Business or trade. The Secretary of Commerce helps the President with problems of *commerce*.

committee—A group of people picked to do a definite job. We are on the party *committee*.

compromise—When people cannot agree — Each gives up something so that both sides get something more important. We had to *compromise* to pass the Constitution.

Congress—The group of people who make our country's laws. The Senate and the House of Representatives are the *Congress* of the United States.

constitutional—A law which is legal according to the Constitution. The Supreme Court declared the law to help the workers *constitutional*.

Court of Appeals—A court that hears cases which are appealed from the district courts. Ms. Anderson appealed her case to the *Court of Appeals*.

dictator—A head of a country who has all of the power. We are thankful that we do not have a *dictator* in this country.

150

display—To show. There are rules on how to *display* the flag.

District Court—The lowest court in the federal court system. Federal cases start in the *District Courts*.

document—An important paper that tells about an agreement or something to be noticed. The Constitution is a wonderful *document*.

domestic tranquility—Peace at home or in our country. The police make sure that we have *domestic tranquility*.

elastic clause—The section of the Constitution that gives Congress the power to pass laws on things that are not mentioned in the Constitution. The *elastic clause* is used to pass laws on modern things.

electoral college—A group of people who select the President by counting the electoral votes from each state. The *electoral college* is not a school.

electoral vote—The vote by state for President and Vice President. John F. Kennedy won the *electoral vote* to become President.

enforce—To see that something is carried out. The President's main job is to *enforce* the laws.

enumerated powers—Things Congress can do that are clearly written in the Constitution. The power to print or coin money is an *enumerated power* because it is written in the Constitution.

federal government—Our country's government. The main offices of the *federal government* are in Washington, D.C.

foreign—Any country besides our own. Cuba is a *foreign* country.

freedom—When you can decide what you want to do. We have *freedom* of speech in this country.

grand jury—A special jury that sees if there is enough evidence to accuse someone of a crime. The *grand jury* did not charge Mr. Jones with the crime.

house—The Senate or the House of Representatives. These are the two *houses* of Congress.

impeachment—To accuse a President or federal judge of poor conduct. *Impeachment* is done by the House of Representatives.

independence—Freedom. We won our *independence* from England.

interpret—To tell the meaning of. The Supreme Court *interprets* the Constitution.

judicial review—When judges interpret the Constitution. They decide on what they believe the writers of the Constitution meant. *Judicial review* keeps our Constitution modern.

jury—A group of ordinary citizens who decide who is telling the truth in a case. The *jury* found the woman innocent.

legislative—The part of government that makes the laws. Congress is the *legislative* branch of the federal government.

libel—To write a lie. Mr. Chian sued the newspaper for *libel*.

majority—More than half of something. The *majority* of children do not want school on Sunday.

militia—A military group that protects the citizens of a state. The *militia* stopped the riot.

naturalized citizen—A foreign born person who becomes a citizen. Mr. Sanchez was born in Mexico. He took a special test to become a *naturalized citizen*.

nominate—To suggest a person for a job. Presidents are *nominated* at their party's conventions.

petition—To ask the government for something. The citizens signed a *petition* for a new park.

political party—A group of people who agree in many issues. The Democrats and Republicans are our two major *political parties*.

poll tax—A special tax that must be paid before someone can vote. A *poll tax* is now unconstitutional.

popular vote—The actual vote of the people. The *popular vote* is the number of votes that the people cast.

posterity—The future. We want to save our resources for *posterity*.

power—The ability or right to do certain things. The Supreme Court has the *power* to rule laws "unconstitutional."

preamble—The statement that tells the purpose of the Constitution. The *preamble* was written before the main part of the Constitution.

privilege—A special right given to some people. Senators have the *privilege* of sending mail without postage.

prohibited—Not allowed or not legal. A law which punishes people for what they did before the law is passed is *prohibited* by the Constitution.

proposal—A plan to do something. A *proposal* is the first step in passing an amendment to the Constitution.

pursuit—The search for something. We are entitled to *pursue* happiness

quorum—More than one half of the total membership. A Group. There must be a *Quorum* before the House can vote on a bill.

ratify—To make a proposal official. The states voted to *ratify* the amendment.

rebel—One who fights against their own government. Many of the colonists were *rebels*.

repeal—To cancel or undo. The amendment was *repealed*.

representation—Having somebody in government to look out for you. Congress *represents* the American people.

responsibility—Something that you should do. We have the *responsibility* to be good citizens.

revenue—Money collected by the government. The government gets much of its *revenue* from the income tax.

revise—To change something. The club *revised* its rules.

revolution—A sudden change. Some colonists began to think of a *revolution* to solve their problems.

Revolutionary War—The war that we fought for independence from England. England lost the *Revolutionary War*.

rights—Things that we may do because we live in a free country. Freedom of religion is one of our *rights*.

slander—To say a lie. The bank president sued Mr. Jones for *slander*.

State Department—The President's cabinet department that deals with other countries. The Secretary of State is the head of the *State Department*.

Supreme Court—The highest court in our country. The *Supreme Court* has nine judges (justices).

symbol—A thing that stands for something else. The flag is a *symbol* of the United States.

term—The number of years that a person serves in a public job. A President has four years in each *term*.

trade—Business or commerce. The United States *trades* with Japan.

treaty—An agreement between countries. The Senate must approve of a *treaty* that the President signs.

trial—A case or lawsuit in court. Americans have the right to a fair and speedy *trial*.

unconstitutional—A law which goes against the meaning of the Constitution. The Supreme Court declared the law "*unconstitutional*."

Union—The United States. There are fifty states in the *Union*.

urban—cities or crowded areas — San Francisco is an *urban* area.

vertical—Upright. Up and down. The flag pole is *vertical*.

veto—To vote against. Presidents *veto* bills that they do not like.

warrant—A legal paper signed by a judge. The police have a *warrant* to search Tom's house.

UNITED STATES CONSTITUTION

Test 1

FILL IN THE RIGHT WORD

1. A person must be _____ years old to become a naturalized American citizen.
   - A. 10   C. 18
   - B. 21   D. 5

2. Everybody who lives in this country is either a citizen or

   an _____.
   - A. eagle   C. apple
   - B. alien   D. Eskimo

3. Children under 18 years old who live in the United States are

   _____ if their parents become citizens.
   - A. aliens   C. poor
   - B. adults   D. citizens

4. An alien must know about American history and the

   _____ to become a citizen.
   - A. Constitution   C. rules for driving a car
   - B. Greek language   D. name of a lawyer

5. We are _____ until we are proved to be **guilty**.
   - A. jailed   C. angry
   - B. innocent   D. taxed

6. The President is the _____ of the Executive branch.
   A. sponsor   C. helper
   B. leader   D. soldier

7. Congress passes _____ that it wants to be laws.
   A. bills   C. days
   B. contracts   D. memos

8. After Congress passes a bill, the President _____ it if the President wants it to be a law.
   A. notes   C. files
   B. signs   D. rejects

9. The President is _____ of the armed forces.
   A. Commander-in-Chief   C. sergeant
   B. mascot   D. mayor

10. Treaties are _____ signed by the United States and another country.
    A. warnings   C. invitations
    B. agreements   D. pieces

11. The flag is a _____ of our country.
    A. symbol   C. picture
    B. copy   D. cartoon

12. A _____ is a legal paper signed by a judge which gives permission for the police to search a house.
    A. warrant   C. magazine
    B. book   D. jury

13. A person must have a fair and _____ trial.
    A. speedy   C. televised
    B. private   D. slow

TRUE OR FALSE?

Circle T or F:

14. An alien is always a creature from outer space.   T F
15. Puerto Ricans are citizens of our country.   T F
16. A person who wants to be a naturalized citizen of our country must speak perfect English.   T F
17. All persons born in the United States are citizens.   T F
18. People who win their court cases cannot be tried again for the same crime.   T F
19. A person on trial is guilty until proven innocent.   T F
20. Congress may not collect an income tax.   T F
21. A president may have five terms in office.   T F
22. Judges interpret the Constitution.   T F
23. The federal government and the state governments share some powers.   T F
24. Someone who robs a bank in California and runs to Nevada cannot be punished for the crime.   T F
25. State laws must agree with the United States Constitution.   T F

UNITED STATES CONSTITUTION

Test 2

CIRCLE THE LETTER THAT TELLS THE RIGHT ANSWER

1. Our country's first constitution was the:

    a. Declaration of Independence.
    b. Articles of Confederation.
    c. Magna Carta.

2. Which of these countries did not have any colonies in the new world?

    a. China.
    b. France.
    c. Spain.

3. The main reason that the colonists were angry with the English was:

    a. The English tea was not good.
    b. The taxes were too high.
    c. Their were not enough parties.

4. Article I. of the Constitution is about the:

    a. President.
    b. Congress.
    c. Supreme Court.

5. A United States senator's term in office is:

    a. Six years.
    b. Four years.
    c. Two years.

6. A President's term in office is:

    a. Four years.
    b. Two years.
    c. Six years.

7. A United States Representative's term of office is:

    a. Four years.
    b. Six years.
    c. Two years.

8. What is the name of the building in which Congress meets?

    a. White House.
    b. Capitol.
    c. Supreme Court.

9. Which of these is one of the "houses" of Congress?

    a. Supreme Court.
    b. Senate.
    c. President.

10. Which branch of our government runs the courts?

    a. Legislative.
    b. Executive.
    c. Judicial.

TRUE OR FALSE?

Circle T or F:

11. The President may make a law without Congress.   T F
12. The elastic clause stretches the power of Congress to make laws.   T F
13. If people lose their cases in court, they may get another chance to appeal.   T F
14. Each state has two members in the Senate.   T F
15. The Supreme Court can make laws.   T F
16. The first ten amendments to the constitution are called the Bills of Rights.   T F
17. A compromise is a way to settle an argument.   T F
18. A jury decides who is telling the truth in a trial.   T F
19. The President is the leader of Congress.   T F
20. A President must be at least 35 years old.   T F